WHEN THE FINAL WHISTLE BLOWS

WHEN THE FINAL WHISTLE BLOWS

Glory, Grief and Tottenham Hotspur

ANDREW PETTIFER

Copyright © Andrew Pettifer 2025
First published by Hembury Books in 2025
hemburybooks.com.au
info@hemburybooks.com
Paperback ISBN 9781923517011
Ebook ISBN 9781923517004

The moral right of the author has been asserted.
All rights reserved. No portion of this book may be reproduced in any form without permission from the author and publisher, except as permitted by Australian copyright law.

 A catalogue record for this book is available from the National Library of Australia

IN LOVING MEMORY

*Dedicated to Cameron 'Commander' Whyte,
a passionate Spurs fan and loyal friend to many.*

As always, "Come on you Spurs!"

Contents

Preface ix

Prologue xi

Chapter 1 — August 2024: Optimism and Nostalgia 1

Chapter 2 — September 2024: A Chronic Condition 9

Chapter 3 — October 2024: Only Spurs... 25

Chapter 4 — November 2024: Yo-yos and Roller Coasters . . 39

Chapter 5 — December 2024: Are You Not Entertained? . . . 53

Chapter 6 — January 2025: Diminished Jeopardy 75

Chapter 7 — February 2025: Punditry and Leadership 97

Chapter 8 — March 2025: A Stay of Execution 117

Chapter 9 — April 2025: Dignity or Silverware 129

Chapter 10 — May 2025: The Final Whistle Blows 149

Epilogue 169

Also by Andrew Pettifer 171

Acknowledgements 173

About the Author 175

Preface

I conceived this book to tell the story of a football season through my eyes, written week by week as a contemporaneous record. Hopelessly optimistic, I resolved to record the emotional journey of fully committing to Tottenham Hotspur and their Australian head coach, Ange Postecoglou. I was convinced it would be a joyous and successful season. In the end, I was right. And yet also, as the story ultimately veered from football to the essence of life itself, sadly wrong.

Everything changed late in the season when I received a call from Jason Whyte to update me on the situation with his brother and my good friend, Cameron. Known to fans in Sydney as our 'Commander', Cam was the leader of the Sydney chapter of OzSpurs, the official Tottenham Hotspur Supporters Club of Australia. It was a role he held for eight years, most of which was time he spent battling cancer. Jason's call was to tell me that the end was in sight. Cam was in the Chris O'Brien Lifehouse Hospital.

The end of Cam's life was a lesson in how to die with dignity. In a remarkable fluke of timing, it coincided with the end of both the English Premier League season and the trophy drought that blighted Spurs for 17 years. Spurs won the Europa League trophy four days before Cam died through voluntary assisted dying. That feels like a trivial detail, when taken in the context of the end of a 65-year life. But it brought happiness to Cam in his last days.

Visionary Founder of the Lifehouse, Chris O'Brien, had a saying. "Everyone needs hope. We live on hope."

Hope is a theme I wrote about when I started the book, in relation to following a football club:

They say it's the hope that kills you. I don't believe that's true. It's the hope that sustains you... The hope may die, but we all know it will be resurrected in only a few short months, as the prospect of a new season brings fresh optimism.

For Cam, there won't be a new season. But his memory will be kept alive by his many friends in OzSpurs who live on with hope. The hope that we will see more nights of glory like the one that marked the end of Cam's days. And the hope that, when the whistle finally blows for each of us, we can learn from our Commander and face that day with grace and dignity.

This book is dedicated to Cameron Whyte. Our Commander. COYS.

All proceeds from this book are being donated to the Chris O'Brien Lifehouse for cancer research, in memory of Cameron and in recognition of the first-class service they provide for the people of Australia.

Prologue

August 2024

I cried out in anticipation. It was precisely one second before Lucas Moura scored the decisive goal in Amsterdam, capping off his stunning hat trick and sending Spurs to the 2019 Champions League final. Video evidence bears witness to my actions; a rare and prescient moment of clarity. The term 'limbs' might have been coined for what followed: 'fans going absolutely mental, much more than a usual celebration'. Grown men embraced strangers and danced on tabletops, as beer rained down around them.

This scene didn't take place in North London, nor in The Netherlands. It was 16,630 km away in The Surry Hills Hotel, Sydney, and it was breakfast time. Alongside me, hundreds of Spurs fans packed into the bar, home of the Sydney chapter of the Australian Spurs supporters' club 'OzSpurs'. The feeling of pure joy that goal engendered sent the assembled throng off to their workplaces with springs in their steps. Some celebrated by jumping into the harbour alongside the iconic Sydney Opera House, to the bewilderment of early-morning joggers and tourists.

For the final, the same venue hosted an all-nighter ahead of the 4am kick-off. I arrived at 11pm to soak up the atmosphere and mingle with fellow Spurs fans. The whole place was festooned with Tottenham Hotspur regalia, whilst highlights of former glories played on the big screens. By kick-off, the place was heaving. It was a lock-out. Stewards turned disappointed fans away to seek other venues. Some stood on the street, peering through the window in an attempt to catch a glimpse of the game. We lost, of course. This is Spurs I am talking about.

All organisations have their own culture and Tottenham Hotspur's centres on the concept of glory. It's an interesting word. Definitions include such elements as honour, beauty and achievement. It has a prominent place in the Tottenham Hotspur lexicon. "Glory, Glory, Tottenham Hotspur", "The Game is about Glory", and my personal favourite: "It is better to fail aiming high than to succeed aiming low. At Spurs we set our sights very high, so that even failure will have in it an echo of glory." That last one, attributed to former player, manager and club legend Bill Nicholson, is most relevant to the current generation. Because, infamously, Tottenham Hotspur fans have been experiencing failure consistently for quite a while now. Sixteen trophyless years. For a club whose Latin tagline is 'Audere Est Facere' – to dare is to do – there's been a lot of audering and not much facering.

Thinking about the culture at Spurs reminds me of my career journey as a consulting engineer. I became fascinated by the concept of an organisation's culture and how a good one, established and promoted through effective leadership, creates success. I ultimately summarised my recipe for leadership as: hire brilliant people, create an environment in which they can flourish, and glow in the reflected glory of their achievements.

Translate that simple recipe into what went on at Tottenham Hotspur under the three previous head coaches and the problem becomes clear. Creating an environment in which the team can flourish should mean being true to the culture of the club. Glory! The last three head coaches were so lacking in ambition to play with honour, beauty and ultimately achievement that we might characterise them as inglorious. Nuno, Mourinho and Conte – the Inglorious Bastards!

The fortunes of Tottenham Hotspur matter to me not only because I am an OzSpurs member and Australia-based Spurs supporter. Tottenham is where my mother grew up. It's where my father took me every other Saturday during my formative years, a football club that I have followed for my whole life, since 1965. Which makes the season ahead – 2024/5 – the 60th of my life. Season 60.

I don't recall the first few seasons of my life, although Dad leaving home at about 2pm every other Saturday through the season is something I was always aware of. Those were the days when all First Division matches kicked off at 3pm on a Saturday afternoon. In the UK, the BBC showed highlights on Match of the Day on Saturday evenings, and ITV showed other matches on The Big Match every Sunday lunchtime. As a child, I lapped it up.

In the early seasons, the winning of trophies seemed quite normal.

Season 2 – FA Cup winners

Season 6 – League Cup winners

Season 7 – UEFA Cup winners

Season 8 – League Cup winners

Season 10 was my first year as a season ticket holder. Season 12 ended in the despair of relegation, and season 13 in the joy of promotion. Then came the 'I was there' trophy seasons, when I attended the victorious finals.

Season 16 – FA Cup winners

Season 17 – FA Cup retained

Season 19 – UEFA Cup winners

Things then became a bit sparse.

Season 26 – FA Cup winners

Season 34 – League Cup winners

Season 43 – League Cup winners

And then, nothing. Zero. Crickets. Those 16 trophyless years, and counting.

That last trophy arrived in 2008, just one year after I emigrated from the UK to Australia.

They say it's the hope that kills you. I'm like Ted Lasso though. I don't believe that's true. It's the hope that sustains you. It's the hope that puts the spring in your step on the first day of the season. It's the hope that brings supporters together all over the world, at whatever time the television moguls declare appropriate. And, for Spurs supporters, it's the hope that withers and dies, along with the cup exits, and the Premier League aspirations as they turn from plausible, to unlikely, to mathematically impossible. The hope may die, but we all know it will return in only a few short months, as the prospect of a new season brings fresh optimism.

There's an oft-quoted saying that the definition of insanity is doing the same thing over and over again and expecting a different result. Or I think of the behaviour of caged animals, repeatedly exhibiting a sequence of movements. Pointless, achieving nothing, drifting into insanity. Have we, the Tottenham Hotspur supporters of the world, become institutionalised, driven insane by 16 years of repeatedly hoping, and failing, to witness the desired outcome?

I guess it depends on what you believe the desired outcome is. We have the best stadium, the best training facilities, and we have secured our position in the 'big six'. For the owners, we have created a lot of wealth. The foundations have well and truly been laid. For the fans, though, the currency of success is silverware. All we need is for someone to come along and create the winning culture that will ultimately break the trophy drought. And I believe that man has arrived. To the great delight of those of us who prosecute our support through OzSpurs, he has appeared in the unlikely guise of an Australian. From the humble origins of a career starting in Melbourne, a serial winner has emerged. A winner in the A League, the J League, the Scottish Premier League and the Asian Championships: Ange Postecoglou. Born just 37 days after me in the summer of 1965, it's his Season 60 too, and his second as Head Coach at Tottenham Hotspur. Finally, Spurs supporters have a leader we can believe in.

My wife Tracy and I have left behind our full-time work careers to travel. We have drawn up our bucket list of places to visit, things to do. When in Australia we live in our motorhome, sharing our time between our family-owned caravan park at Gilgandra in Regional New South Wales and the open road, exploring our adopted country. In the Australian winter months, we chase the sun to the northern hemisphere.

Wherever I am, and whatever I am doing, there is a constant that travels with me. It's the next Spurs game. Where will I be, how will I get a live feed and at what ungodly hour will it be happening? This book documents a season in which I am going all-in, through an unrequited relationship with fellow Aussie Ange Postecoglou. A contemporaneous record, compiled through the season, exploring the emotional landscape that full commitment reveals, intertwined with the stories of a life of full-time travel. The story of a season that will surely see a trophy arrive at Tottenham Hotspur Stadium. With Ange at the helm, one thing is for sure, it's going to be a hell of a ride. Buckle up…

Author's note: What you have just read was written before the season started. What follows was written week by week, as the season progressed. Each chapter is a month and each subheading denotes a new week. Because of this, the end of each week is written in the present tense, whilst the week I have looked back on is in the past.

CHAPTER 1

August 2024: Optimism and Nostalgia

... And Leicester!

"We all follow the Tottenham, over land and sea... and Leicester!" Spurs supporters have sung, for as long as anyone can remember, for reasons that nobody seems to know. Except that Leicester is a nondescript city somewhere between the north and south of England. Certainly not the sort of place that would produce a Premier League winning team. Until 2016 that is, when they did just that, having been offered at 5,000/1 by bookmakers at the start of the season. Who's the joke on now?

It was an appropriate place to start, because following Tottenham Hotspur over land and sea is what this book is about. For this first match of the season, though, Tracy and I were in physical attendance. Our life of travel takes us away from Australia to avoid the winter down under and embrace the northern hemisphere summer. Which is why we were in the UK as the new season kicked off. In Leicester.

I'd not been to Leicester before, but in the short time we were there I got to know it well. One particular part, at least. Repeatedly we circumnavigated a one-way system looking for the car park I had pre-booked, the street signs seemingly mocking us as we searched for a clue to our intended destination. Misguidedly, we put our faith in technology to direct us. You'd think we'd have learnt from the time Apple Maps sent us down a pedestrian only street in Verona, the terms 'UNESCO World Heritage' and 'Low Traffic Zone' evidently having evaded its attention. Hordes of tourists surrounding the entrance to Juliet's balcony parted in our path like the Red Sea, as locals took out their phones to alert the authorities. It's a long bow to draw between Leicester and Verona, I know. But I'm sure, like the Veronese, the good people of Leicester love their city, even if it wasn't immediately evident to us why. World Heritage it certainly isn't.

As a child, I didn't attend many away games. Mainly I'd be at home games, sitting in the old West Stand at White Hart Lane alongside my dad. We'd stamp our feet to make the wooden stand rumble whenever Spurs won a corner and, at half-time, cigars would be lit by the gentlemen around me. It was obvious to me why we were called Yids. Even now, the smell of cigars reminds me. From my cosseted position, the prospect of mixing it with the throng on the terraces looked a bit scary. I do remember being on 'the shelf'– the terrace where the most raucous supporters would congregate – for the semi-final of the UEFA Cup, in 1984. The noise was intense and the proximity of strangers, singing at the tops of their voices and swaying in unison, somehow both intimidating and joyful. A rare away excursion was at West Ham. I recall going through a makeshift metal detector to be greeted by Nazi salutes from those in claret and blue. That really was scary. Some of my peers still romanticise that era, but I'm firmly in the pro-gentrification camp. Give me a padded seat and a salmon and cream cheese bagel over a concrete terrace and fascist mob, any day of the week.

As it turned out, being in the away end at Leicester felt more like the 1970s than the gentrified 2020s, except the metal detector is now a hand-held wand. A particularly inebriated Spurs supporter and his mates did a good job of spoiling everyone's enjoyment, swearing loudly and invading the personal space of whoever had the misfortune to be in their proximity. The stewards ignored them, fearing a confrontation. Most took pleasure in singing obscenities. Heaven knows what the young couple from South Korea sat next to me made of it. I'm hoping their limited English spared them the Spurs fans' grotesque opinion of Jamie Vardy's wife, infamous star of the 'Wagatha Christie' controversy.

Monday, August 19th 2024. King Power Stadium, Leicester, England.

Premier League: Leicester City 1 Tottenham Hotspur 1

Ange picked a side that was largely familiar from the previous season, except with Solanke starting as the great new hope at centre forward. Unsurprisingly, the match played out as many did last season, with a strong start undermined by a poor second half. The absolute dominance that Spurs had over Leicester during the first half took us into half-time with a 1–0 lead, and a false sense of confidence that we would push on to a comfortable victory. The supporter standing next to me was clearly a seasoned Spurs fan and expressed the view that one goal was a slender lead that could easily be lost. Which is exactly what happened when Vardy, clearly past his best but still giving it a go, found himself unmarked a few yards from goal. A cross sailed over the hopelessly mis-positioned Romero, reached Vardy's head and was dispatched past a flailing Vicario.

Alarmingly, the concession of the goal seemed to panic the Spurs players, who started to look second best. A wholesale change of the midfield by Ange, including new signings Gray and Bergvall, steadied the ship and demonstrated the depth of the squad that the summer signings had created. With no further goals, the home crowd greeted the final whistle with delight and the Spurs fans bemoaned a result that should never have been. Contrasting emotions then, from the two sets of supporters.

To experience a range of emotions is integral to the human condition, although I suspect that is not something your average football supporter spends a lot of time thinking about. Undoubtedly, they experience emotions in abundance. It's what being a supporter is all about, although being a Spurs fan brings its own complexities. Most top clubs' supporters experience the joy of winning trophies every now and again. Even less fancied clubs like Leicester, as their fans took delight in reminding us, and West Ham, have had recent silverware to celebrate. Not Tottenham Hotspur. To be a Spurs supporter, I always say, builds emotional resilience. We experience more sadness and disappointment than joy and victory. At least in the big important games, and oftentimes in the games we should win, like away to a newly promoted Leicester City.

Over the years, I have come to manage this predicament by tempering my emotional response.

"Why don't you seem bothered when they lose?" Tracy would ask.

Well, I admit, it was a defence mechanism. One thing I have learnt in my near 60 years is that you can play down your emotions to cope better with the lows, but if you do so, don't expect to fully experience the highs. So this year, when I believe Ange will bring home the silverware, I resolve to be open to fully enjoying the experience. I'm putting my emotional wellbeing firmly in the hands of Tottenham Hotspur and, specifically, Ange Postecoglou. Psychologists call this being a 'highly identified' fan. And the good news is that research shows highly identified fans benefit from their role in the fandom, experiencing high social self-esteem, and low levels of loneliness and isolation. Bring it on!

The disappointment of the result at Leicester doesn't feel too painful. I saw a lot that I liked. I'm naturally an optimist, and I'm looking forward to the long season ahead.

Rolling Back the Years

Being a Spurs supporter was never a conscious decision for me, it was a birthright. A life sentence, some might say. The genesis of this allegiance was when my dad, as a young lad, was offered the opportunity to go to a match by his uncle.

"Do you like blue or red?" he was asked, to which my dad replied, "Blue." Had he not, I would today be a supporter of that other North London team – Woolwich Wanderers (or Arsenal, as they are sometimes known).

Virtually all football clubs, like Tottenham Hotspur, stay true to their geographical roots. Every now and again, a team decides to relocate, like Wimbledon moving to Milton Keynes. It's never a good thing. Woolwich decided in 1913 to relocate to North London and, like a cuckoo, came into Spurs' nest and has made a nuisance of itself ever since.

My dad bought me my first Spurs season ticket for my 10th birthday. It was the 1975–76 season. Before that, he went with a couple of friends, one of whom would only decide on the morning of the game if he was using his ticket that day. If he decided not to, he would call to say that I could go in his place. I would spend my Saturday mornings sitting by the phone, desperately hoping for it to ring. Often, it did.

The name on my first season ticket was Mr Hardy, curiously Dad's was Mr Harvey. This was because in those days there was a long waiting list for a season ticket. When someone decided to give theirs up, rather than give it back to the club, they would pass it on to a friend and simply notify a change of address, retaining the name that was on the ticket. When the West Stand was rebuilt in 1982, the club announced an amnesty and invited season ticket holders to notify them of their real names. Around 70% had to be changed.

Many older Spurs supporters recall that era with the sepia tint of nostalgia. They don't remember, or choose to forget, how poor the team was. Even with genuine club legends Pat Jennings, Glenn Hoddle and Steve Perryman in the team, Spurs narrowly avoided relegation in 1975–6 with an end of season 4–2 victory over reigning champions

Leeds United. That night was the most exhilarating atmosphere I can remember at the old ground.

It was the match when winger Alfie Conn at one point sat on the ball, an act of gamesmanship and a demonstration of showboating for which any player today would be heavily criticised. Which feels like a shame. Conn himself says he did it to "take the sting out of the game," or, in common parlance, waste time. Despite only narrowly escaping relegation, courtesy of that famous victory, the players are feted as greats of the past. Except for the three aforementioned, they weren't great. They were, for the most part, ordinary at best. This was confirmed the following season, 1976-7, when Spurs finished bottom of the league and finally experienced the ignominy of relegation.

I am reminiscing about going to Spurs as a young lad because our travel plans changed to accommodate a Scandinavian cruise before our return to Australia. As a consequence, the window of opportunity opened for me to do something that I'd not done for over 40 years – go to a home game with my dad.

One of the reasons Tracy and I chose to leave behind full-time employment and embrace a life of travel was to be able to spend more quality time with our parents in the UK. My mum was uneasy about travelling alone with my dad, worried something might go wrong while they were overseas. Our return flights to Australia were flexible, and we had no firm commitments to return for, so we came up with a plan. We would extend our stay to travel with them.

A cruise departing from Southampton, not far from their home in the New Forest, turned out to be the perfect option. With no flights needed, it made an easy start and end to the journey. The only cruise that fitted the bill was scheduled to set sail during the week after the first home match of the season, a Saturday clash with Everton. It felt like the stars had aligned. To mark my dad's 86th birthday, I decided to buy us both tickets for the game.

With it being a last-minute decision, all the general admission tickets had already been sold. But as Australians like to say, no dramas. I've come to realise that you can find a way into just about any event, as long as you're prepared to part with enough cash. When the occasion is big enough, and your wallet allows it, you can make it happen. Tottenham Hotspur chairman, Daniel Levy, is well aware of this, of course. Which is why there are so many 'premium experience' seats at the stadium.

With two of these overpriced tickets tucked into my digital wallet, we left the New Forest and pointed the car towards North London. I'd debated whether to go by train or drive, park at Wood Green, and hop on the complimentary shuttle bus that the club provides. That option had served us well before but, sadly, not this time. The classic British summer was out in full force. Relentless rain and slick roads meant traffic jams all over the place. What should've been a breezy two-and-a-half-hour journey dragged on for a frustrating four. We'd given ourselves more than enough time to enjoy the perks of the premium package, but that time was spent inching along the North Circular, rain streaking the windows and Radio 5 Live keeping us company.

> **Sunday, 24th August 2024. Tottenham Hotspur Stadium, London, England.**
>
> **Premier League: Tottenham Hotspur 4 Everton 0**
>
> After that unfortunate start to the day, I needed Spurs to step up and put in a good display in recognition of our historic father-son day out. This they did with a dominant victory. It was an enjoyable watch, and a comfortable one. Spurs supporters are used to living on their nerves. As the Leicester game had demonstrated, a 1–0 lead is not enough. But, at home to a weak Everton team, a blistering shot from Bissouma and a Sonny steal from the blundering Everton goalkeeper Pickford,

> had us two up in 15 minutes. From that point on, the result was never in doubt. Other highlights of the match were an excellent debut by winger Odobert, and a barnstorming run by Van De Ven (hereafter referred to as VDV) to set up the fourth goal, Sonny's second of the match.

I was at the first home game of the previous season too, a 2-0 win over Manchester United, describing it thus:

The euphoria that I felt at the conclusion of the match was palpable around the whole ground. This was not a crowd simply celebrating a good home win. There was a genuine sense of joy tinged with relief. The cognitive dissonance that we have collectively felt in recent times as supporters of a club that expounded one philosophy but practiced another has dissipated. We have our club back. Glory is back on the agenda.

This time the atmosphere in the stadium was more one of satisfaction than excitement. I see this as a significant accolade for Ange. After a year of his management, exciting attacking football is now not, in itself, something to celebrate. It is expected. A 4-0 win against a weak opponent is simply a good day at the office.

An enjoyable and nostalgic day out and I'm feeling happy with our start to the season.

CHAPTER 2

September 2024: A Chronic Condition

A Familiar Toon

Since its inception in 1992, the English Premier League (EPL), born out of the old English First Division, has been on a mission to capture the attention of sports fans around the world. It's been a resounding success. A global audience in the billions makes the league the most popular sporting competition on the planet. This was brought home to me on a visit to Peru, earlier this year. An hour's drive and a two-hour boat trip from civilisation, we stayed at a research lodge in the depths of the Amazonian rainforest. Our local guide noticed me wearing a Spurs shirt.

"Tottenham Hotspur," he exclaimed in his broken English, "Good team." I agreed. "Son," he informed me, "Great player!"

When I travel to other parts of the world, I like to connect with local supporters. The global nature of the Spurs family, and the unerringly positive greetings that overseas visitors receive, always make for an enjoyable experience. I've attended meet-ups in San Francisco, Singapore and New Delhi, as well as multiple locations across Australia. The Tottenham Hotspur website now has a searchable map showing the locations of literally hundreds of supporters' clubs all over the world. There's even one in Peru. Under the 'About Our Club' section, it simply states 'We are based in Peru'. Not all that helpful for any intrepid traveller hoping to meet up with Peru Spurs to watch a game.

Scandinavia has long been a hot spot for Spurs supporters. I have distinct memories of busloads of Scandinavian tourists arriving at White Hart Lane in the seventies and into the eighties. In 1982 Norway was the second overseas supporters' club to be formally recognised by Tottenham Hotspur, after Malta.

On the day of the Newcastle match, our cruise ship, Celebrity Edge, was docked in Stockholm. The Swedish Spurs supporters' club claims on its website to number 1,750 members, and I imagine that number is growing. For the first time in history, two of the star players of the current team are Swedish – Kulusevski and Bergvall. Previously only one Swede had represented the club at the highest level – Erik Edman, a left back who played the 2004/5 season. Whilst Mr Edman's contribution was limited to one season, the highlight was quite remarkable – a 35-yard screamer at Anfield that rivals even Victor Wanyama's famous strike into the same goal, 13 years later.

I'd have loved to meet up with the Swedes to watch the game, but 'all aboard' for our ship coincided with kick-off at 2.30pm local time. Having checked my ability to stream the game through the ship's WI-FI, my streaming service and judicious use of VPN, I discovered that Premier League screenings are provided as part of the cruise ship's entertainment offering. And so, as the ship pulled out of port to negotiate approximately 24,000 islands that make up the Stockholm archipelago, Tracy and I settled down on the top deck. Wrapped in blankets to protect us against a chill sea breeze, we watched the match unfold on a giant screen, accompanied by a small smattering of fellow passengers.

Two hours later, our sense of early season anticipation and optimism was in tatters.

Sunday, 1st September 2024. Celebrity Edge, Stockholm, Sweden.

Premier League: Newcastle United 2 Tottenham Hotspur 1

We were without Solanke up front again. After playing a full season for Bournemouth, he took a knock in his first Spurs game and was out for weeks. More importantly, VDV was missing from the defence. It's too early to know what impact Solanke will make, but we already know how reliant we have become on VDV. With a system of play that often exposes us to counter attacking threats, the team relies heavily on his speed to get us out of trouble.

Ange's tactics are inherently positive, relying on a high press and attacking prowess to overload the opposition and score freely. Even if we defend mostly with only two at the back, and concede the occasional goal on the counter, we trust we are going to score more. That is, after all, the point of a game of football, to score more than the opposition. It's a style that fits well at Spurs. As club legend Danny Blanchflower said, "It is about doing things in style, with a flourish, about going out and beating the other lot, not waiting for them to die of boredom." Sadly, despite some style, and much flourish, in this match we again failed to capitalise on these qualities.

Having thrashed Leicester 1–1 in our opening away game we had now played Newcastle off the park for a 2–1 defeat. It had turned into a distinctly 'Spursy' start to the season. Like many Spurs supporters, I don't like the word, but it's entered common parlance, defined in the Urban Dictionary as "to consistently and inevitably fail to live up to expectations. To bottle it."

With my newfound resolve to fully engage this season, I am contemplating my feelings about these early setbacks. I'm undoubtedly disappointed, a little sad, although not overwhelmingly so. Quickly I move to rationalising the situation, allowing my intellect to manage my emotional response. This ongoing struggle between cognition and emotion interests me. I observe this dynamic in myself and in others. How the two interact is a determining factor in personality and behaviour, and it is written clear in supporters' reactions to football matches.

Some say, "It's early in the season. We are dominating matches. Our new centre forward is injured. We just need to take our chances. In Ange we trust!"

Through social media, we can quickly see the reactions of others, for whom emotion appears to override reason. "We have no centre forward! Our signings are shit! We can't defend! Ange doesn't know what he's doing!"

These diverse reactions extend beyond mere opinions; they reflect a deeper theoretical discourse; the process by which people seek to create and shape truths through their interactions. Each says something about the author of the post. Their psychological state, their worldview and how they want to be perceived. Which begs the question, what do my reactions say about me? I am, at least for now, in the rationalising camp. But is that simply protecting me from confronting the full emotional range that I have committed to? Am I at some level avoidant, inadequate even? Maybe it's too early to say. Sit with it, as the therapist might counsel, and see what comes up.

It's frustrating to have two weeks to wait for the next match, courtesy of the international break. It'll hopefully mean that we have a fully fit squad for the game. The small matter of a home North London derby.

Joy and Pain

The saturation coverage of EPL now available in Australia is a far cry from the turn of the century. A small group of fans, including Justin Long, a Sydney based expatriate Londoner with a passion for Spurs, had the idea of coordinating supporters around the country and establishing a national supporter's club in Australia.

"We got TV advertising on Sky when they hosted the EPL, identified suitable Spurs fans in other states and asked them to make a 'chapter'. Perth was first after Sydney and then it rolled out nationally," Justin tells me.

One early Aussie supporter was then 13-year-old schoolboy, Tommy Silver.

"The internet was still in its infancy, and I was a budding web designer, so I wrote to Justin to ask if I could make a website for OzSpurs," recalls Tommy, now an IT professional based in Japan. (On Spurs 2024 pre-season tour to Japan, it was Tommy that Tottenham Hotspur turned to as translator when the local fans engaged with the Spurs hierarchy, including Daniel Levy, Ossie Ardiles and Ledley King.) "The website was launched in late 2001. I'm proud to say it was a big hit, coming right at the perfect time as the Premier League was seriously taking off in Australia. It played a major role in bringing all the OzSpurs chapters together and becoming the official Australian supporters' club in 2003."

Fast forward 20 years and OzSpurs is, in my view, the best overseas supporters' club in the Spurs global family. I say this not just because it is my 'home' club but because it operates on a federated model, with a national committee co-ordinating the local chapters. With 11 chapters established, in all major urban centres across the country, OzSpurs is the most extensive English Premier League supporters' club in Australia.

I remember the day I first crossed paths with Justin and Tommy like it was yesterday. It was 17th November, 2012. I had been thinking of going to an OzSpurs event for a year or two so when I spotted a golf day advertised on the club's Facebook page, I finally decided it was time to sign up, and I went along.

It was a bright, crisp spring morning at Moore Park Golf Club. A crowd of mostly middle-aged men, decked out in Spurs gear, gathered over bacon rolls and tea. I was put in a four-ball with Justin. We stood at the first tee, surveying the fairway ahead and taking in the unmistakable scent of newly mown grass. Chatting came easily. We were expat Brits, united by geography, circumstance, and a deep connection with Tottenham Hotspur.

That round of golf was just the start of what turned into a memorable day. Afterwards, I strolled across the road to the Sydney Football Stadium to meet my daughter, Anna. That evening, we were swept up in the magic of a Coldplay concert. I remember the moment Chris Martin shouted, "turn on the lights now, let's go!" Everyone's wristbands lit up in sync with the music, and the entire crowd became part of the spectacle. They still do it at their shows today, but that evening it was the surprise of not knowing it was coming that made it such a memorable moment.

After seeing Anna safely home, I moved onto the Surry Hills Hotel, then known as the Triple Aces Bar, to watch the North London derby. This is when what had up to that point been a wonderful day headed south, and fast. In what many Spurs fans will recall as an iconic match, Emmanuel Adebayor (former Woolwich player who had switched to playing for Spurs) scored the opening goal in the 10th minute and was sent off in the 18th minute. Cue the flood gates opening and we were 3–1 down by half-time, at which point I gave up for the night, exhausted by the day's events. But the day didn't end there. Tracy, a relatively new girlfriend at the time, was overseas on business, and I had borrowed her car for the day, a silver convertible Audi A3. Driving home with the roof down enjoying the warm night air was always likely to attract the attention of the police manning a random breath testing station on Military Road.

"Just count to ten," said the police officer, waving a probe in my face. This might be the easiest test I ever pass, I thought to myself, confident in my sobriety. The police officer held me in position longer than I'd expected and started to wander around the car, tapping on his device. "This car doesn't appear to be registered sir, is it yours?"

"It's my girlfriend's," I said, "I'm sure it must be." It was the moment I discovered Tracy was not across her domestic paperwork, and the responsibility for making sure a vehicle is registered is the driver's, not the owner's.

"You're going to have to leave it here until you can get it registered," I was told.

As I walked home from Spit Junction that night, I reflected on a memorable day of highs and lows. The final scores: Coldplay 10/10; Woolwich 5, Tottenham Hotspur 2; NSW Police 1, Me 0.

Since that initial engagement with the OzSpurs community, I have become a regular attendee at match meetups in Sydney and 'Nationals'. The National is an annual event where supporters from chapters across the country come together for a weekend. The host city varies each year. I have attended Nationals in Sydney, Melbourne, Adelaide, Brisbane, Perth, Newcastle and Cairns. They're always fun events and a chance to catch up with Spurs friends, new and old.

Naturally, the National includes watching a match, although on one occasion the television schedule scuppered a Brisbane weekend by moving Spurs' game to a Monday night, missing the planned weekend altogether. We went ahead anyway. Since then, Nationals have taken place on the last weekend of the season, this being the one match we know won't move to suit the television schedule. All matches in the last round of the season have to start at the same time, on the same day. This season, the National will be in Sydney. It's where this book will end. I doubt we will celebrate success in the Premier League, but the

FA cup final is 6 days before the Sydney National is due to start and the Europa League final is the morning of the day before. I can see the 2025 National being extended should we be in either, or even both. The way things have been going in the early part of the season, I won't be extending my Airbnb booking just yet.

Currently, our itinerant lifestyle limits the number of meet-ups Tracy and I can attend in person, but our arrival back into Sydney from Europe coincided with the weekend of the home North London derby. As Tracy and I entered the Surry Hills Hotel, we encountered a few familiar faces and many new ones. About two hundred Spurs fans had gathered to commune, drink beer and experience the match together. The atmosphere was raucous, with occasional outbursts of terrace songs becoming more frequent as game time approached. I can report that Sol Campbell and Arsene Wenger remain unpopular.

Our collective experience watching the game brought to mind that we had, during the international break, lost one of the last great soul singers, Frankie Beverly, from the group Maze. This might be deemed ironic, at least to The Guardian journalist whose report on the game described how, "Tottenham's attempts to find a way through the Gunners' defence at times resembled the efforts of a particularly dim-witted lab rat trying to negotiate a maze."

The actual reason I mention the late Mr Beverly's demise, other than as a tribute to the man who I first saw perform in Paris in 1985, is because the group's best-known hit, 'Joy and Pain', seems so appropriate to the experience of devoting yourself to Spurs.

And the North London derby certainly was painful. Not in an acute 'dagger to the heart' kind of way. Our pain is long term, our suffering a chronic condition.

Sunday, 15th September 2024. Surry Hills Hotel, Sydney, NSW.

Premier League: Tottenham Hotspur 0 Woolwich Wanderers 1

Early phases of the match flattered to deceive. We had by far the most possession. The high press yielded some half chances. As the match wore on however, it became clear that Woolwich had a tactical plan, founded on a strong defence and a confidence that they could let us have the ball and not be too troubled by what we were going to do with it. As The Guardian maze analogy highlighted, the Spurs attack was full of running, but lacking in goal scoring prowess. Solanke, we can forgive for still settling in. Johnson consistently fails to impress, and Sonny blows hot and cold. The inevitable concession from a corner left us looking clueless in the final flourishes. The Sydney OzSpurs dispersed into the night to once more nurse our chronic conditions, at 1am Australian east coast time.

I don't know if Ange is a fan of Maze, but he certainly understands what Beverly's lyrics were saying. Here's a quote from an early Spurs press conference in which he declared his role is to bring joy to the fans: "And joy comes from suffering... It is not about being happy, because you actually suffer a game of football until the ball goes into the net, or you win the game. I want to bring them joy, but they need to understand there will be some suffering with it."

Following an underwhelming start to the season, there were many questions to be asked about the challenges facing the team and the prognosis for the season ahead. But I was not about to give up on Ange only four games in. Yes, it hurt, and for sure, I was concerned that my commitment would bear more pain than joy. But then as Frankie and Ange have both reminded us, joy and pain... they're both one and the same.

In Ange's post-match interview following the Woolwich defeat, he doubled down on his comments that he 'always' wins a trophy in his second season, and expects to do so again. It was hence with an air of anticipation that Spurs fans looked for what the starting team would be for the mid-week visit to Coventry, in the Carabao Cup.

> **Thursday, 19th September 2024. Gilgandra Caravan Park, NSW.**
>
> **Carabao Cup: Coventry City 1 Tottenham Hotspur 2**
>
> Ange chose a second-string line-up, leaving in three players from the Woolwich game – Udogie, Bentancur and Solanke – presumably to play them into form.
>
> Having mastered the art of dominating a match and failing to win in the previous weeks, this match saw something different. Playing badly and winning. In a display of breathtaking ineptitude, we made a championship team look like worthy winners before two late goals secured the victory, and a place in the next round. In a further twist, the winning goal was a deft one-touch over the keeper from Brennan Johnson, a man much pilloried following the Woolwich game and only on the pitch because of an injury to Odobert earlier in the match. The assisting pass was Bentancur's first meaningful contribution, two minutes into added time at the end of the game.

Ange's words about suffering a game of football never rang truer.

Angeball Returns

In the aftermath of games, I listen to a Spurs fan podcast. It's a good way to test personal reflections against those of others and, particularly following a loss, process the pain. It's football supporter therapy.

There are many Spurs podcasts available, but my preference is The Cheese Room, named after the apocryphal fromagerie claimed to have been planned at the new stadium. The club has denied such a plan ever existed, but the story lives on in the pod's name. I first became aware of The Cheese Room through fellow Sydney OzSpur Aaron Jolly, bon viveur turned devoted father, and a co-founder of the podcast. Being a frequent traveller, the global nature of the production appealed to me. The format includes three podcasters discussing the previous game, at least one of whom is normally outside of the UK. Contributors are regularly from North and South America, Europe and occasionally Australia. Sometimes we hear from former OzSpurs president Paul 'PAF' Fellowes. I like to hear considered but impassioned discussion and I don't want to listen to emotion laden rants, or overly technical analysis. The Cheese Room strikes the balance well.

Listening to the edition following the Woolwich loss was confronting. Not so much from the discussion about the game, which aligned with my own thoughts, but from the analysis of Ange's record as Spurs manager. Regular contributor Seb Short analysed Ange's results over the previous 32 matches, since last season's infamous loss at home to Chelsea, and compared them with a similar number of matches under Conte and Mourinho, prior to their sackings. They were remarkably similar. In short, we concede too many, don't score enough, and as a result don't win many games. If the season carries on in the same vein, we will end up around 12th in the league. Conclusion: something needs to change.

With my natural sense of optimism duly dented by this statistically undeniable analysis, I was looking forward to matches with a sense of trepidation. It wasn't supposed to be like this. It's Ange's second season. Surely he will win something. I'm recording it all for posterity, to allow fellow Spurs fans to relive the season, because this is the year things are going to come good! Don't let me down Ange, it's time to turn things around.

Sunday, 22nd September 2024. Gilgandra Caravan Park, NSW.

Premier League: Tottenham Hotspur 3 Brentford 1

Having only just recovered from jet lag, I succumbed to the prospect of a 2am bedtime to watch the latest instalment in our chequered start to the season live. It was midnight on the east coast of Australia as the Brentford game kicked off and, 23 seconds into the new day, we were 1-0 down. But fear not, Ange had answered my call. I'd almost forgotten what the much-vaunted style of play that has come to be known as Angeball looks like, but here it was in full flight. In possession, play is fast tempo, direct and brave. When the ball is lost, what in basketball they would call a full court press is applied; attackers and midfielders, even the full backs, press to win the ball back quickly and as high up the pitch as possible. Defensively, we play a super high line, leaving space behind and backing our defenders to sweep up when the opposition counter. It's still frantic in defence, but chances are created, risks are taken and we're backing ourselves to win by outscoring the opposition. Against Brentford, we did just that. A tap-in for Solanke restored parity with his first goal for the club, and a precisely struck shot from Johnson put us into the lead after half an hour. The fear of a late dose of Spursiness leading to another disappointment was apparent in the stadium as the game wore on, but a well worked late goal from Maddison put the game, and me, to bed.

Going straight to bed at 2am after watching an exhilarating game is not conducive to sleep. Inevitably, it takes time for my mind to stop racing. During that time, I contemplate what words I might use to describe what I have just watched. On this occasion, one word kept coming up: manic. The Dutch invented Total Football, Ange seems to have created Manic Football. I'm not sure that mania is the key ingredient for winning the Premier League, I imagine Ange would agree. A little more control is required, particularly at the back and from goalkeeper Vicario, the most manic of the lot. Never mind, for now the emotional rollercoaster was climbing rapidly, and surely Thursday's game against Qarabag would only maintain the upward momentum.

It's in Azerbaijan, you know. I admit I had to Google it. They play in Baku now, the country's capital, after being displaced during the First Nagorno-Karabakh war, which took place between 1988–1994. Having to look these facts up reminds me I'm ashamed of my lack of historical knowledge. Not surprisingly, my knowledge of the First Nagorno-Karabakh war was non-existent. Likewise, the Second Nagorno-Karabakh war which, I was surprised to discover, happened in 2020. Under the cover of Covid, whilst we were all busy baking cakes and learning how to do Teams calls, Azerbaijan won a war. I imagined a team coming from such a troubled part of the world would be no pushover. They've also won nine of the last ten Azerbaijan Premier Leagues, which makes them the Manchester City of Azerbaijan, but without the (alleged) 115 counts of cheating.

Friday, 27th September 2024. North Ryde, Sydney, NSW.

Europa League: Tottenham Hotspur 3 Qarabag 0

Ange chose an exciting blend of youth and experience for the match. With Romero suspended for a long forgotten previous misdemeanour, Dragusin partnered VDV in the centre of defence. But not for long. In an unexpected early turn of events, the Romanian committed the sin of a drag back on the opposition's centre forward, simultaneously performing his own name in a game of football player charades and receiving his marching orders. Udogie replaced the dejected Bergvall, and the team performed a kind of self-healing wound for the rest of

> the match. If it weren't for the little red icon in the corner of the screen, you'd not have known we were one man down. Another neat finish from Johnson, a goal from a corner by Sarr and a tap in from the impressively industrious Solanke completed a comfortable victory.

The Azerbaijani's were, in the end, more war torn than battle hardy.

We Have Lift Off!

"The journey is the reward." – Chinese proverb

For lifelong supporters of a football club, the long and winding journey through life is accompanied by the annual sojourns that each season takes us on. Over time, the cycle of seasons becomes familiar and comfortable, like an annual trip to the seaside. Even for Spurs fans, who have become accustomed to the journey stopping short of the intended destination, the trip feels worthwhile. A glimpse of the ocean, but no ice cream.

I must confess that my interest in the proverbial seaside jaunt has not been consistent through the 60 seasons of my life. Having witnessed the cup successes in the 1980s, my passion waned, as my career and young family became a priority. Living on the South Coast took me more often to watch Southampton play. It was close to where I lived, and my business had season tickets for entertaining clients. Under Gordon Strachan, Southampton was playing a brand of football far more progressive and successful than Spurs. In the FA Cup third round of 2003, Southampton played Spurs off the park for a 4-0 victory. The Tottenham Hotspur news archive describes the game as 'desperately disappointing'. Southampton lost the final in Cardiff that year. It pains me to write it: 1-0 to... you know who.

For many years, my life journey was fairly conventional. School, university, professional career, wife, two children (George arrived in 1996 and Anna in 1998), mortgage, dog. All that was to change when my then wife Wendy and I started looking at moving away from the New Forest to somewhere that would provide more opportunities for our children. The answer, as it turned out, was further afield than we had imagined. Sydney.

In 2007, I was recruited into a senior role at the Sydney office of Arup, the global consulting engineering firm that first went to Australia when they designed the structure of the Sydney Opera House. Paul Sloman was the guy responsible for hiring me, a 'Gooner', would you believe? Now a good friend, we have an annual wager of a slab of beer on who will end up higher in the league, meaning I've been topping up Paul's beer cellar for the last few years.

2011 was a pivotal year in my life. My first marriage ended, I took some time out and learnt a lot about myself before, later in that year, meeting Tracy. We were married in 2016. To say Tracy has changed the trajectory of my life is an understatement. She has made me a better person and joined me on a path that is far less conventional. Which, in a roundabout way, is how I ended up in a motorhome parked up in our own caravan park at Gilgandra, Regional NSW, about 500 km from Sydney, watching Spurs play Manchester United.

Monday, 30th September 2024. Gilgandra Caravan Park, NSW.

Premier League: Manchester Utd 0 Tottenham Hotspur 3

Manchester United away is not a game that has historically borne much fruit. Normally they are a good team, but now, with Erik ten Hag in charge, things are different. This time, we put in a dominant display and achieved a comfortable victory. Our season is finally in full swing, and we are playing a thrilling style of football! VDV set the tone for the day in only the third minute with an interception in his own half and a run to the byline to set up a tap-in for the resurgent Johnson. Yes, get in! The full court press worked its magic again against a dithering United defence, creating more chances. A turning point in the game saw the dismissal of Bruno Fernandes for a foul on Maddison. If the referee had an orange card, he probably would have shown it, but with the choice between yellow and red, he chose the latter. A harsh call. Spurs scored again early in the second half through Kulusevski, his first goal of the season, and the team went into game management mode. A limited rally by United created some discomfort, before a Solanke goal from a Sarr flick-on at a corner put matters to rest.

Following the return of Angeball against Brentford, we finally have lift off. How do I feel? Bloody marvellous! Even so, a question lingers in the back of my mind. Was that a superb Spurs display, a demonstration of the power of Angeball on one of the biggest stages in world football? Or did we simply take advantage of an abject performance from a proud club that has lost its way? United, as the brilliant Phil McNulty wrote for the BBC, "started dreadfully and went into rapid decline." The Spurs fans rubbed it in, serenading ten Hag with the "Sacked in the morning..." taunt.

CHAPTER 3

October 2024: Only Spurs...

Back to Earth

Later in the week, Spurs travelled to Ferencvarosi, Hungary's most popular team. Like Tottenham Hotspur, they have a new stadium – Ferencvaros Stadion, a modest 22,000 community facility. Unlike at Tottenham Hotspur, Beyonce has not performed there. Even more unlike Tottenham Hotspur, they've won the country's top professional league, the Nemzeti Bajnokság, for the last six seasons. This makes them the Manchester City of Hungary, but without the (alleged) 115 counts of cheating. Hungary's response to Covid was less radical and more peaceful than that of Azerbaijan, although it did involve the declaration of a state of emergency and, for the benefit of those at home baking, the announcement of Hungary's cake of the year for 2020; Curiositas. Aptly named, presumably a decision arrived at over a Teams call.

Friday, 4th October 2024. Gilgandra Caravan Park, NSW.

Europa League: Ferencvarosi 1 Tottenham Hotspur 2

Ange again chose a team blending experience with youth for this second Europa League game. His strategy is becoming clear. Use these matches to give the young players first team experience, but include enough senior players to guide them and give confidence that we can win the game. Pack the bench with the rested senior players and bring them on late in the game to shore things up, or turn them around, as needed. This game saw starts for both Moore and Lankshear in the forward line, joining Gray and Bergvall as the teenage contingent. All did well, particularly Gray, who, unusually, played at centre back in the first half, then swapped with Davies and played left back in the second. What looked like a comfortable victory, with goals from Sarr and substitute Johnson, felt slightly Spursy with a late goal from the home team, but the game was adequately managed to a conclusion.

That's five wins on the bounce since the North London derby.

Winston, as we have named our motorhome, is an Avida Longreach. Colloquially referred to as a Winnebago, the American equivalent. Ten metres in length, and with two slide-outs to increase the internal area when parked up, Winston is a one-bedroom apartment on wheels.

When we're not out exploring with Winston, he's parked up at Gilgandra Caravan Park. It's our home base in Australia whilst we are travelling. Back in 2018, we bought the caravan park business as a family venture with Tracy's son, Peter, and his wife, Katie. They've made it their permanent home, where they are raising our two grandsons. The park provides them with employment, a home, and six acres of open space for the boys to roam and play in. This week we returned there for some down time following our overseas trip.

Winston is equipped with all the facilities I need to watch the matches, as and when I choose. That I can watch all Premier League and European competition games, on multiple devices, wherever I am in Australia, live or whenever I wish, is thanks to a range of technical innovations and no little expense. Firstly, Starlink, a super-fast mobile internet service which is all about satellites, and something to do with Elon Musk. It's not cheap but provides download at over 100 MB/s and upload at around 30MB/s anywhere in Australia. I also pay monthly charges to various streaming service providers. Three different providers hold the rights to the EPL/FA Cup, the European competitions and the Carabao Cup. It doesn't seem right or fair on the customer, but that's how it is. You pays your money and you makes your choices. Although, in truth, not that much money. The Premier League and FA Cup rights are owned by Optus, the country's second largest telecoms company. Because I also use them for my mobile phone service, I pay $9.99 per month for every Premier League and FA Cup game, live, 'on demand', or neatly served up as 3, 9 and 25 minute highlights packages. That's about the cost of two large coffees per month. Some Australian fans still complain about the cost, but UK fans could only dream of such a deal.

After the North London derby, Brennan Johnson received a lot of abuse online and took down his Instagram account. Keyboard warriors are a curse of modern life and Spurs fans contain their fair share of them. Online abuse of anybody is abhorrent, however privileged and wealthy they may be. My own comment after the Woolwich game was that "Johnson consistently fails to impress". I recall also saying to the supporter standing next to me in the pub that I thought Johnson was simply not good enough to be in the team. Both of those comments were measured, fair and critical. Since then, he has scored in five games in a row and could have had more. The team playing the way Ange wants them to has shown why he rates Johnson. He does exactly what is asked of him in the system, which is to be in the right place at the right time, to score goals. Fair play to Johnson and Ange. The other thing I want to highlight is that with this story of the season being written contemporaneously, week by week, I'm not going back to edit earlier chapters to look smart with the benefit of hindsight. Like any supporter, I have opinions that shape my perspective and feed into my emotional journey. Happily, I have placed my emotional welfare in the hands of Ange and, not surprisingly, his judgement is proving better than mine.

Monday, 17th October 2024. Gilgandra Caravan Park, NSW.

Premier League: Brighton and Hove Albion 3 Tottenham Hotspur 2

It was 7am when I fired up the Apple box and tuned into Optus Sport to stream the Brighton game in Gilgandra, four and a half hours after it kicked off on the South Coast of England. An early start ahead of our planned trip to the Gold Coast with Peter, Katie and the boys during the school holidays. Blissfully unaware of the result, I was feeling confident that the upward trajectory of the season would be maintained. At half-time we were 2-0 up and, whilst not having had things all our own way, a sixth win in a row looked assured. I took a shower whilst the half-time analysts did their thing and contemplated another fortnight of contentment ahead, during the international break. As it turned out, 8am was the high point not only of that day, but of the week that followed. In 18 minutes, aided by some calamitous Spurs defending, Brighton scored three times. The confidence did not so much leach out of the Spurs team, as implode like a deflating balloon. Without this key attribute, we gained no momentum, and played with no evident urgency for the rest of the match. Worryingly reminiscent of the Woolwich game, we never looked like scoring once we went behind, and defeat became inevitable.

In my new state of emotional vulnerability, this one felt bad. Really bad. Not just a reminder of the chronic condition, but a genuine blow to the solar plexus. This defeat couldn't be put down to early season settling in, like Newcastle, or the lottery of a North London derby. This was a game we should have won. Confidence was high. I thought we'd won the game at half-time. Maybe the players thought so too. Ange clearly shared the pain, his post-match reaction like that of a parent, not so much angry with the misdemeanours of his children as genuinely disappointed. The pain stayed with me through the day and beyond.

We set off north up the Newell Highway in Winston that morning, confident that he had been fully serviced, new tyres fitted, even his solar system repaired since our last road trip. Three hours later, with Tracy at the wheel, all traction power was lost, and the dash lit up like a Christmas tree. Much like Tottenham Hotspur, whilst the wheels hadn't fallen off, confidence was back to a low ebb and a repair job was required. Winston's fix turned out to be a quick and easy one, once he'd been towed to the nearest Isuzu garage and we'd spent the night on their forecourt awaiting the morning shift. A loose fuel filter bleed valve was the culprit. I fear that no such quick fix lies at Ange's disposal. And, with the international break ahead, it will be two weeks before he can get things back on the road.

Hammering the Hammers

Stretching south from Brisbane along Queensland's southeastern edge, the Gold Coast is a ribbon-like city hugging the shoreline. According to Queensland Tourism, it boasts "over 70 kilometres (44 miles) of golden beaches, perfect waves, and breezy seaside bars." What the brochures don't mention is the never-ending sprawl of apartment towers, strung together by congested dual carriageways. A concrete scar across what was once a pristine stretch of coast.

Our visit to the Gold Coast brought to mind the saying 'it never rains but it pours', both literally and figuratively. The following day, more heavy rain cut short our afternoon at SeaWorld, one of the many amusement parks drawing visitors to the region. Even the sea lion show was called off because of the weather. For safety reasons, they said, though it wasn't clear whose safety they were worried about.

Things went from soggy to sour the next morning. Since late last year, we'd had two e-bikes chained and clamped to the back of the

Suzuki, which we tow behind Winston. While we were staying in a rented apartment, we parked the Suzuki and bikes safely in the underground car park. Or so we thought. The rest of the family stayed across the street in Winston at a caravan park. As I walked into the car park the following morning, something wasn't right. I soon realised what it was. No bikes.

Around the back of the car I could see the chains had been cut clean through, clamps forced apart, and the bikes stolen. Welcome to the Gold Coast, home of sun, sea and stealing. We're told the criminals here are as high as the tower blocks, and even more offensive.

The theft was a further blow to the solar plexus, worse than that caused by the recent Spurs capitulation. It wasn't the cost, or even any attachment we had to the bikes. It was the feeling that we had been personally violated, through the proxy of our possessions. This was turning into a very bad week.

The feelings that this trauma brought up made me question my response to the debacle at Brighton and contemplate what having an emotional engagement with a football club means. Is it really that important? That millions of people around the world are passionately engaged despite, or maybe because of, the everyday traumas that life presents them, must mean something. The thought went to the back of my mind as we planned the next step on our journey.

It is a sign of the strength of OzSpurs that there are chapters not only in the main urban centres but in some of the smaller cities. Keen to leave the Gold Coast as soon as Peter, Katie and the boys headed home, we travelled south down the coast in time to meet up with the Newcastle chapter of OzSpurs for the West Ham game. Tracy and I were warmly welcomed at the Wests Leagues Club by long-term chapter organiser Shawry, and a handful of Novocastrian Spurs.

Shawry is one of many friends I have made over the years through

OzSpurs. In Sydney, the chapter used to be led by Cameron Whyte until poor health prevented him from continuing. Cam, affectionately known as 'Commander' for his rabble rousing calls to arms on Facebook, is Australian. When I asked him how he got into supporting Spurs he said that a friend had suggested it to him in the playground at school one day and he'd gone with it. That he developed such a passion for the club from that simple beginning, through all the adversity of being a Spurs fan, speaks to the character of the man. As loyal a friend as anyone could wish for.

Other good OzSpurs mates include Nathan Pieterse, the new Sydney Chapter leader, former club Presidents Paul 'PAF' Fellowes and Mark 'Paxton' Lawson, Graeme 'Jockney' Anderson from Adelaide, Kevin 'Woody' Woodward from Cairns, Emma-Jane 'EJ' Stephenson from Melbourne... and too many others to mention. What I love about this cohort of friends is that if it weren't for OzSpurs I wouldn't know any of them. It's a melting pot of good people with a shared passion for Spurs and a willingness to put that before anything else.

Shawry explained to me about the Newcastle venue where we had arrived to watch the West Ham game. "We used to meet in a local pub with a bit more character than this place," Shawry explained. "But Covid, a change of ownership and repositioning of the establishment into a 'gastropub' put paid to that." And so it was that we met in a typical Australian club environment, making up for what it lacked in character with multiple huge television screens, and a wide range of cold beers.

Saturday, 19th October 2024. Wests Leagues Club, Newcastle, NSW.

Premier League: Tottenham Hotspur 4 West Ham United 1

The West Ham game was a welcome return to winning ways. Despite conceding first, the team rallied strongly, winning thirteen corners before Kulusevski struck the equaliser, in off both posts, late in the first half. Kulusevski's form in the attacking midfield role has been a highlight of the season so far. A player with great awareness, touch, strength and finishing, he is proving a handful for all opponents. A blistering eight minute spell early in the second half saw us 4–1 up with goals from Bissouma, Sonny and a welcome donation from one of the West Ham defenders. The Hammers' best player and goalscorer, Kudus, finished the game with what we used to call an early bath. After twice kicking VDV on the ground, he followed up with a slap to the defender's head when he got up to protest. Remarkably, this was followed by a palm to the face of Pape Sarr. Three red card offences in quick succession were met with a yellow card by the hapless referee before VAR did its job and the red card was finally produced. After the week we'd had, this win felt like a welcome tonic. There's a feeling not only of joy but also optimism, when the team plays such dominant football. Surely it's only a matter of time before we are doing this every week?

My education of second tier European competition teams to be found in the Europa League continued later in the week when we played AZ. Cunningly known by just two letters, their name gives little clue to their origins until Google revealed they stand for Alkmaar Zaanstreek. Being from The Netherlands, there are no Covid wars to report, but I discovered they were the team that lost to Ipswich in the 1981 UEFA cup final. It was a two-legged affair which took place on either side of the FA Cup final and replay of the same year. Having been at both of the FA Cup finals (in season 16), and witnessing the greatest cup final winning goal of all time, by Ricky Villa, I believe I can be forgiven for forgetting that Ipswich won the UEFA cup in the same year. Let alone that a Dutch team known simply by the first and last letters of the alphabet were their opponents.

Friday, 25th October 2024. Gilgandra Caravan Park, NSW.

Europa League: TH 1 AZ 0

Ange made nine changes from the West Ham game. Any fears of a Coventry style performance proved unfounded and, in a relatively uneventful encounter, a 1–0 victory was secured through a Richarlison penalty. Undoubtedly, the highlight of the evening was the performance of Mikey Moore. After the withdrawal of Werner at half-time, Moore switched to his preferred left side from where he ran the AZ defence ragged for a 20 minute spell, including the move that led to the penalty. Werner, by contrast, performed poorly, demonstrating a lack of confidence in front of goal to squander two good chances. A misplaced pass directly to a red shirt with no colleagues in the vicinity would have caught Ange's eye just as much.

If we are going to build a team that can challenge the three front runners in the Premier League – Manchester City, Woolwich and Liverpool – we need all our players to be, or have the potential to be, good enough for their squads. By that measure, Werner is nowhere near good enough. Most fans and commentators believe this performance will be the nail in the coffin for Werner's Spurs career. Personally, I'd put Richarlison in the same category, although the chances of finding a top class striker who is willing to play second fiddle to Solanke is slim. It feels disloyal to question the capability of our players in this way, but it's not a popularity contest and, unlike at my grandson's under eight's team, there are no prizes for participation.

Two good wins to get us back on track following the Brighton debacle and I'm feeling confident going into the weekend fixture against a Crystal Palace team that hasn't mustered a single win this season. To be followed by a League Cup tie against a Manchester City team that, in contrast, hasn't lost this season.

It's a Process…

Watching the West Ham game at the Wests Leagues Club reminded me of the central part gambling plays in Australian society. Clubs like Wests are found in all Australian towns and suburbs. Many have a name usage agreement with the local Returned and Services Leagues (RSL) veterans' association, others are sports based clubs, known as 'Sporties'. Nearly all of them rely on 'pokies' – slot machines in the UK – for income. They also provide opportunities to gamble on what seems to be an endless stream of horse and dog races from all over the world, shown on multiple screens. As we travel around the country, we observe how many racecourses there are, often found in small towns. Gilgandra has one, just over the road from our caravan park. Remarkably, Google advises that there are 367 in all.

I have mixed feelings about gambling. Tracy and I quite enjoy a flutter to add a bit of interest when we are watching sport. I rarely bet on a Spurs game. I really care about what happens and the winning of a few dollars doesn't make any difference to my level of engagement. There's a case for betting against Spurs, to at least get some compensation should we lose, but that feels disingenuous. And I'd have to cover off both a loss and a draw, which wouldn't be worth doing.

I'm well aware of the social damage done by gambling. In Australia, it's as big a problem as it is anywhere. I've personally known people whose lives have been ruined. There are regularly stories of gambling related suicides in the media. Mostly, these are associated with pokies, machines that are literally programmed to encourage addiction. Why governments allow this reveals their priorities in stark terms, measured in dollars and cents. Tax revenues from pokies in the current year will be around $1.5 billion in NSW alone.

Ultimately, whilst greater regulation and limits on the more insidious forms of gambling would be welcome, I believe we have to accept it. There are many things that do damage in our society which we accept and manage. Heading a football, to take a relevant example, over time causes brain damage and risks early onset dementia. It's proven, but we don't stop people doing it. Tobacco, alcohol, sugary drinks, fast food, the list is long.

Whilst tending not to gamble on our matches, I should share that I have bet on Spurs winning a trophy this year, because I believe that is what will happen. It is, after all, Ange's second season, and he's promised. Not literally, but that's how I have interpreted his words.

Monday, 28th October 2024. Gilgandra Caravan Park, NSW.

Premier League: Crystal Palace 1 Tottenham Hotspur 0

Back on the pitch, our yo-yo start to the season continued with a 1–0 defeat away to Crystal Palace. I should have felt a gut-wrenching sense of disappointment, but in truth, I didn't. Despite my commitment to putting my emotions on the line, I struggled to really feel anything other than a depressing sense of familiarity. This wasn't even a case of Spursiness, which would have required us to look like we might get something from the game before failing at the last. No, this was the first game in the season where I felt we deserved nothing from our performance. Palace out-pressed us. We struggled to pass out from the back and when we did, they quickly sat into a low block. When we are playing well, it looks like we have more players on the pitch than the opposition. On this occasion, it felt like the opposite. Surely any hope that we might mount a challenge for the title has well and truly disappeared with this defeat.

Ange tells us it's a process. It would appear to be one that will take more than two seasons, although I'm not writing off the prospect of him taking us there, eventually. Even the best managers can take a few seasons to reach peak influence. Manchester United, for example, were initially inconsistent under Alex Ferguson's guidance, finishing in 11th, 2nd, 11th, and 13th places in what was then the First Division. I still have faith that we will win a trophy under Ange this season. On our day, we can beat anyone. For now, though, I am resigned to us being a cup team. In truth, that is what we have been for all of my sixty seasons. You have to go back to my dad's generation to find people who remember us as title winners.

After ruminating over the Palace defeat, Tracy and I, spending a few days in Sydney, walked from our city centre Airbnb to the Surry Hills Hotel to watch the Carabao Cup tie against Manchester City. It was our first return there since the defeat in the North London derby. With 7.15 am kickoffs like this, the pub shows its commitment to OzSpurs by opening their doors, although at this time they sell very little to the assembled diehards.

The history of the establishment's relationship with OzSpurs goes back to the early days of the club. The founders of OzSpurs wanted to find a pub that would host meetups and literally walked the streets of the city looking for one that would agree. What was known then as The Triple Aces, a pub on Elizabeth Street, close to Central Station, agreed. It is a fairly typical inner city pub, with the front bar resembling a betting shop, and a smoking room full of pokies at the back. In between, though, is where the magic happens. A bar with three large television screens, a Tottenham Hotspur themed pool table, Spurs memorabilia on the walls and a space large enough to accommodate a couple of hundred fans or, on this occasion, precisely eleven.

Thursday, 31st October 2024. Surry Hills Hotel, Sydney, NSW.

Carabao Cup: Tottenham Hotspur 2 Manchester City 1

My prediction that we had seen the last of Timo Werner proved to be wide of the mark when, with Sonny still injured, he appeared in a reasonably strong line-up named by Ange. In a development reminiscent of my earlier misplaced judgement on Johnson, Werner swept in the opening goal of the match within six minutes of play. The bright start continued when an exquisitely curled shot from Sarr crept inside the post for 2-0. Inevitably, City started to find their rhythm and, with Spurs desperately trying to protect the two goal lead up to half-time, they drew one back in added time.

During the second half, it felt like the Sword of Damocles was hanging over us, the equaliser and an excruciating penalty shoot out inevitably about to blight our day. My heart rate was raised, adrenal glands fully engaged. Tracy could barely watch. And then, surprisingly, joyously, the final whistle blew. Whilst City did not have their strongest team out, with Haaland left on the bench throughout, they were still a very strong opponent and this felt like an important result for Ange. The victory left us still in the running for four trophies.

This was a week in which we'd followed up a loss against a team that hadn't won all season with a win against a team that hadn't lost. Only Spurs…!

CHAPTER 4

November 2024: Yo-yos and Roller Coasters

Top Scorers!

Whilst we do have a few female members of OzSpurs, notably long-term club stalwart and committee member Emma-Jane Stephenson, it is rare for men to arrive at meet-ups with their partner in tow. In Tracy though, I am very fortunate to have a partner who indulges my commitment to Spurs so completely. When we first met, she had little interest in football.

"The last time I went to a football match, it was at Anfield and John Toshack was playing," she informed me. Over time her interest in, and knowledge of, all things Tottenham Hotspur has grown to where she would consider herself a supporter. In truth, she is a supporter of me, a Spurs fan by marriage.

Tracy is the sort of person who makes an impact wherever she goes and whatever she does. A self-declared control freak but, on the flip side, a brilliant problem-solver, she is a woman of action and a natural leader. Many of her former colleagues have explained to me what a positive influence she has had on their lives, not only their careers. Tracy's own career has been hugely successful. After talking her way into her first job in pharmaceutical sales, she became so effective that the company gave her the role of training all the other salespeople. Further progress led to senior HR roles and, after emigrating to Australia in 2008, a CEO role in a fast growing and successful technology company. In 2016, the Australian Institute of Management named her NSW Leader of the Year. It is more through the success of Tracy's career than mine that we can take time out to travel and tick off our bucket list.

An architect I knew professionally once asked me, when I mentioned that our apartment next to where he lived was bought from the proceeds of Tracy's business interests, how I felt about the fact that my wife earned more than I did. Which I felt was a particularly stupid question, on more than one level. I assured him I was OK with it.

Tracy's mother Elaine, living in Leigh between Manchester and Liverpool, has a disability that requires full-time live-in care. It is a constant source of stress for Tracy to keep close to her condition, ensure her needs are being met, and manage her affairs. The guilt she feels is a common experience for expats. We leave our home country for a better way of life, often taking our children with us. Rarely do parents follow. We rely on visits and video calls to stay in touch. All of which works fine until the going gets really tough.

For Tracy, not to mention Elaine, it became particularly tough a couple of years ago. Elaine's primary carer at the time was, shall we say, unconventional? If you've seen the film 'The Intouchables ' (and if you haven't, you should), you will be familiar with the loveable rogue, played by Omar Sy, who became the carer of a wealthy quadriplegic. Like that character, DW (as I will refer to him) brought fun and laughter to the role. Far more than simply meeting Elaine's basic care needs, he made sure that she was entertained. He organised parties at her house, invited her friends and catered the event. He brought her on holidays to meet us in Singapore, and in Australia. He was great. Until he wasn't. He didn't so much fall off the wagon as hurl himself from a high-speed train. By the time we found out about the problem, he had stolen over ten thousand pounds in cash and most of Elaine's jewellery to feed what we subsequently discovered were serious drug and gambling addictions.

For fear of impacting any future prosecution, I should say that is our allegation. The police's response and subsequent actions were frustratingly slow, but persistent. Nearly two years on, police have gathered sufficient evidence to make a case for a prosecution, but the files have not yet gone forward to the crown prosecution service (CPS). It's been like following a crime series that you're part of, with episodes being released sporadically and with no warning. We expect to have progress to report during this season but a prosecution, and (we hope) a custodial sentence, will more likely come later.

Tracy has supported my passion for following Spurs by joining me at matches when we are in the UK, and becoming part of the OzSpurs family in Australia. Whilst she enjoys going to games, or meeting up with our OzSpurs mates in the pub, when I get up early in the morning to watch the previous night's game, Tracy rarely joins me. I'm sure she looks up the result but knows better than to let on whilst I am watching the game. Which is why, back in Winston at Gilgandra for the Aston Villa game, I was suspicious when I got up to watch the match and found Tracy joining me for the second half. If there was anything to deduce from this, it could only be positive. And so it proved.

Monday, 4th November 2024. Gilgandra Caravan Park, NSW

Premier League: Tottenham Hotspur 4 Aston Villa 1

In a match remarkably similar to the West Ham game, our early industry was nullified by a well-organised opponent. Late in an evenly contested first half, the visitors took the lead from a corner. There's been much discussion about our ineptitude at defending corners, not least from the boys on The Cheese Room podcast whose post-match analysis suggested that we need to find a new goalkeeper for next season. Harsh, I felt, but certainly there's room for improvement. As the podders pointed out, our problem with corners also extends to the other end of the pitch. Our high tempo offensive play and full court press elicits many attacking corners, which should be a potent offensive weapon. Alas, they are either taken short and peter out, or land straight in the hands of the opponent's goalkeeper.

We went in at half-time, still one nil down. A front-footed start to the second half saw a wicked cross from Sonny turned in by Johnson, fast becoming a goal machine, this being his seventh of the season. A bold move by Ange, to the obvious consternation of our captain, saw Sonny substituted for the ever energetic but erratic Richarlison on 55 minutes. Tracy, by this time ensconced beside me, poked fun at my dissatisfaction with Richarlison's introduction. In a display that seemed to sum up his whole Spurs career in one 20 minute spell, he ran around a lot, committed a couple of fouls, gave the ball away three times, assisted a goal for Solanke with a cross and in the process pulled his hamstring. It was then a second for Solanke, who had by this point put us into the lead, receiving a superb through ball from Kulusevski before chipping it over the onrushing keeper. To top things off, and match the 4–1 scoreline against the Hammers, late substitute Maddison scored direct from a free kick on the edge of the box. Remarkably, this was the first goal scored by Spurs from a direct free kick since 2019. It brought our tally for the season to 23, making us top scorers in the Premier League up to this point.

With wins orchestrated against two of the most highly regarded coaches in the Premier League, Guardiola and Emery, this felt like a seminal week for Ange. The boys on the podcast were, I felt, lukewarm in their praise. They haven't quite twigged how good our Antipodean leader is. Ange himself wasn't getting carried away either.

"My eyes are fixed firmly on where we are going," he reminded the assembled press. "If I was a racehorse, I'd be wearing blinkers." I love this guy!

Later in the week, we faced Galatasaray, the first of our Europa League opponents who I had heard of, and could place geographically. It's in Istanbul, a city that I have long wanted to see.

Friday, 8th November 2024. Gilgandra Caravan Park, NSW.

Europa League: Galatasaray 3 Tottenham Hotspur 2

Ange once again put out a half boys/half men team, something of a risk playing away to a formidable opponent who was unbeaten this season. I think the idea is that the men help the boys play like men but, under severe pressure from the outset, the reverse was happening. Perhaps inspired by finding themselves in Turkey, our defence handed out chances like Christmas presents. (Such poor jokes, I imagine, are why the country officially changed its name with the UN to Turkiye in 2021).

Like in the previous Europa League game, the match was most notable for the contributions of one of the academy graduates, this time Will Lankshear. After netting his first senior goal for the club in the first half, a lack of discipline brought about two yellow cards, and hence a red, in the second. 3–1 down at the time, this made it difficult to turn things around, despite Ange sending on a few senior players from the bench. A composed back-heel flick from Solanke got the score back to 3–2, but the winner never arrived and, if truth be told, the scoreline flattered us. I assured myself that the loss probably wouldn't damage our chances of proceeding to the later rounds of the competition and the entire episode could be put down as a great education for the younger players.

Whilst Ange claims not to take too much notice of the league table at this point in the season, the same cannot be said for supporters. Whilst it has felt like a chequered start to the season, the same is true for many clubs. As a result, the fixtures for the week ahead, if they fall in a particular way, could put us third on the table. A draw between Woolwich and Chelsea, defeats for Forest (home to in-form Newcastle) and Villa (away to leaders Liverpool) would only require us to beat the winless Ipswich at home. Our league leading goal difference would then act in our favour. What could possibly go wrong?

Not Again!

As I waited to see whether the weekend's results would indeed see us climb to third on the table, some news came in about our stolen bikes. True to her problem-solving nature, Tracy posted notices of the theft on multiple websites, offering a $1,000 reward for information leading to their recovery. This elicited a tip on Facebook Marketplace stating an address for the criminals, close to where the crime took place. The information was that the address had been raided by the police multiple times for bike theft, and that these people took ours. Whether this was a known fact, or simply a fishing expedition by someone hoping to strike lucky and benefit to the tune of $1,000, we don't know. The information went onto the Queensland Police's database, the case remaining open, although Spurs winning the Premier League feels more likely than us ever seeing our bikes again.

This development returned my mind to the question that was prompted by our unfortunate experience in the Gold Coast. What is it all about, this emotional engagement I, and millions of others, have with a football team?

I've come to learn that the most important thing about life's journey is human connection. And the height of human connection is love, of which I am fortunate to experience much. In Tracy I have found my soulmate. I have my parents, fit and well in their eighties. I have two wonderful, happy, talented and successful 'children' in their twenties. My extended family, in the UK. My 'step' family, including two beautiful grandsons. My close friends in Australia, who we call our 'Australian family'. I am one of a group of eight friends who have known each other since school days. I think one of our mothers gave the group a name, and it stuck: 'The Lads'. Ally, Dave, Graham, John, Doug, Peter, Alex and myself. When we met up at Lords recently for a day at the cricket, I calculated the aggregate number of years of friendship between us to be about 1300. Thirteen centuries of friendship! One of those friends is even a Gooner. He can't help it, Graham's story is like mine, except his dad chose red. My love for all these people, and their health and happiness, are what matter most to me.

"We love you Tottenham, we do...," literally thousands stand together and sing. What is it they love? If I think of the club that I first went to with my dad as a child, there is virtually nothing left. The owners, the players, the stadium, all completely different. Other than a few club legends like Pat Jennings and Martin Chivers, still kicking around on match days, everything has changed. Oh, and the Tottenham High Road, holding back the tide of gentrification that has overtaken much of London. In contrast, how Islington went from being a place to avoid when I was young to some of the most expensive real estate in London in the space of about five years remains a mystery. Particularly given the big new cuckoo's nest that appeared in the area at the time. The whole transformation seems to have been something to do with Tony Blair and 'New Labour', when that was a thing.

What motivates this declared love for a football club? I have two explanations. The first, and most obvious, is the power of the tribe. Supporting a team provides that sense of human connection. Something to have a shared belief in. Football is the religion of our times and stadiums are the cathedrals.

"We love you Tottenham, we do...," means we love being part of this community, our tribe. And it is history that binds the community together; a shared participation in a collective memory bank of cherished moments, and mutual despair. When Jennings and Chivers are no longer around, and the Tottenham High Road has finally met the wrecking ball, we will still talk about where we were when Lucas scored a hat-trick in the Champions League semi-final. Some might even recall that they were the first to cry out in anticipation of the winning goal…

On our travels in regional NSW, we have noticed that the names of some of the non-denominational churches, of which there are many, are based on the notion of hope. 'Community of Hope', is one, 'Living Hope' is another. When I see one, I always say to Tracy, "Just like OzSpurs!" It's become a standing joke, but it's true. The other thing that binds us is hope. One day we will recall how together we endured the trophy drought, and all the success that followed once Ange finally broke it. There's always hope.

For lifelong supporters such as myself, it goes even deeper than that. Being a Spurs supporter is part of who I am. It was preordained. There before my body was formed, let alone my character. Before education, or relationships, or career, or children. In part then, to love Tottenham Hotspur is to love who I am. It represents both my tribe and myself.

And so it came to pass… Chelsea drew with Woolwich, Forest and Villa were both defeated. Third place was there for the taking. And we lost, at home, to the previously winless Ipswich. Yo-yos, roller coasters, bumps in the road. Joy and pain, sunshine and rain. Metaphors and cliches. What is there left to say?

Monday, 11th November 2024. Gilgandra Caravan Park, NSW.

Premier League: Tottenham Hotspur 1 Ipswich Town 2

Ange's approach of accepting risks at the back, whilst relying on turnovers high up the pitch and incisive forward play to create chances, failed again. With VDV injured and replaced by Dragusin, we were too frail in defence, the forwards unable to create enough chances. From 2–0 down, we rallied to get one back. For once a corner found one of our player's heads, rather than the goalkeeper's gloves as it had all afternoon, and Bentancur netted. But there was to be no late redemption and, yet again, we lost a game we should have won.

I'd spent the week re-engaging with Spurs fans on X (Twitter) and found myself in a world of ignorance. Keyboard warriors without an ounce of Ange's experience and knowledge, but with the audacity to question his competence, had me riled. Who are these people? I retorted he would become the most successful manager since Burkinshaw, possibly even since Nicholson. With these exchanges in mind, anger welled up as I sat and watched another defeat to what was clearly an inferior group of players, providing more fuel for the Ange doubters. The reaction to the result on social media included, for many, a discussion on the longevity of Ange's tenure. Opinion became even more polarised between the doomsayers and the committed, the former calling for his sacking, the latter pointing out the absurdity of the notion. If they are true supporters, isn't it their duty to support? In truth, only one man's view matters. My belief that Daniel Levy has learnt from the lessons of the recent past, and is prepared to allow Ange to play the long game, remains steadfast.

What my anger emphasised was that I really am fully engaged this season, not just because I have decided to be for the sake of this book, but because I am a huge fan of Postecoglou. I like that he is Australian. I like that he has come from humble beginnings to reach the pinnacle of his profession, and most of all, I like his leadership style. I have pinned my colours to Ange's metaphorical mast and I'm sticking with him. It was never going to be easy for any coach to turn around the culture of the club, play the football the supporters want to see, and win consistently. It will take time.

Eyes on the long term, blinkers on, trust the process...

In Paradise!

Following the loss to Ipswich and a shitstorm on social media, extended by the international break, Tracy and I treated ourselves to a few days in one of our favourite corners of Australia: Port Douglas. Tucked away in Far North Queensland, it's a holiday hotspot known for its swaying palms, warm tropical air, and easygoing atmosphere. To us, it's simply paradise. I suspect whoever tagged "Far North" onto the name did so to underline just how far it is from some of Queensland's less charming parts. The Gold Coast, for instance. According to Apple Maps, it's exactly 1,834 km between the Gold Coast and Port Douglas. That's over 20 hours by car, or nearly five days on a bike, assuming it hasn't been nicked before you set off.

For the geographically uninitiated, here's a quick rundown of Australia's states: there's Queensland and Victoria, both nods to Queen Victoria. Then there's South Australia and Western Australia, both referencing their place on the map. Oddly, there's no North Australia, but there is the Northern Territory. And there's no East Australia either, but we do have New South Wales, named by Captain James Cook. It's unclear why Cook felt the world was in need of another South Wales. The man himself hailed from Marton, just south of Middlesbrough, so I suppose I should be grateful I don't live in New South Middlesbrough. And then let's not forget Tasmania, although Australians normally do.

The capital, Canberra, sits in the Australian Capital Territory, the ACT for short. It was officially recognised as the capital in 1913, when a competition was held to find a name for the city. The winning name,

'Canberra', was simply an evolution of what the indigenous people had always called the area, 'Canberry'. I guess the white man didn't want the capital to sound like a tin of fruit.

What's less commonly known is that mainland Australia actually has three territories. The tiniest and most obscure is Jervis Bay Territory, or JBT. This little coastal patch, just 67.8 square kilometres in size, was carved out in 1915 to give the Federal Government direct access to the ocean. You would have thought, being the Federal Government, they could access the sea wherever they like along the 27,620 km coastline of Australia, but apparently not.

Back at Port Douglas, thin shards of tropical sunlight pierced the blades of the plantation shutters, waking me at 7am. It was about 90 minutes after the game in Manchester had finished. This was not a match I was looking forward to watching. With City on a run of four defeats, all in away games, a home fixture would surely see a return to form. After all, they'd not lost at home in the Premier League for two years...

Sunday, 24th November 2024. Port Douglas, Queensland.

Premier League: Manchester City 0 Tottenham Hotspur 4

With VDV and Romero both injured, Ange sent out our second string centre back combination of Dragusin and Davies to contain the City attack and Erling Haaland, the Premier League's most prolific goalscorer. Another enforced change resulted from the seven match ban imposed on Bentancur for what at the time I imagine he thought was a lighthearted joke about Sonny, sadly a bad and racially offensive one. Ange made a bold call to move Kulusevski back out to the wing, making way for the return of Maddison. Johnson dropped to the bench.

City spurned several early chances against a decidedly shaky looking Spurs defence. It was thus against the run of play when a long pass out of defence from Dragusin found Kulusevski on the right wing. His raking cross picked out Maddison's run from midfield and a neat side-footed finish put us one up. Not long after, Maddison doubled the lead following neat interplay with Sonny. With Spurs growing in confidence at the back and City clearly rattled, the score remained at 2-0 up to half-time.

The television commentator informing us that City had only failed to score in one of their last 53 home games did nothing to allay my fears that two goals would not be enough.

"We'll need to score again," I said to Tracy, hoping at best for a 3-2 win. When Porro struck our third, after more excellent work from Kulusevski and a lay-off from Solanke, I started to believe the match could go our way. With only a couple of minutes left, I had finally convinced myself that we were assured of victory when a fourth goal arrived, courtesy of substitute 'goal machine' Johnson.

Paradise in paradise – what a scoreline! I was so happy for Ange. This would at least put the doubters back in their place for a few days. Now all we needed was to work out how to beat the teams at the bottom of the league and we would surely make the top four, if not an actual challenge for the title.

Between the Manchester City match on Sunday morning and the Europa League game at home to Roma on Friday morning, Tracy and I went our separate ways. Not permanently, I hasten to add! Ahead of a wedding in our 'Australian family', planned for February, it was time to attend the stag and hen weekends. Anyone who has emigrated to the other side of the world will recognise the bonds that are created with others from your homeland who have travelled the same path. If you arrive in the same place around the same time and with children of a similar age, those bonds become strong and long lasting. Which is exactly how it was when I first met Graham and Nicky, shortly after we all arrived in Australia in 2007. They've been together since well before then, but finally decided to tie the knot.

The ladies took themselves to Noosa on the Queensland coast whilst I jumped in a minibus full of middle-aged men in Sydney and set off for Albury-Wodonga, a town on the NSW/Victoria border. Created in a 1970s style moment of free love between the two states and the Federal government – described at the time as the 'spirit of cooperative federalism' – the city spans the state border, which runs along the Murray River. The intent of the initiative was to encourage decentralisation of the population and the development of an inland city. Quite why that was considered important, when most Australians just want to live near the beach, I couldn't say. Unsurprisingly, the strategy became the victim of a change of government and the aspiration for a city of 300,000 was never realised, the current population being about one third of that. The underlying flaw in the whole plan only really became clear in 2020, when cooperative federalism fell apart in the face of a global pandemic and Victoria closed its borders, leading to mass confusion and delays for ordinary people, trying to do ordinary things, in a divided city.

Friday, 29th November 2024. Lake Hume Resort, Albury, NSW.

Europa League: Tottenham Hotspur 2 Roma 2

Ange chose about as strong a team as he could muster for the Roma game, given current injuries. Sadly, intermittent Wi-Fi and limited mobile reception diminished my viewing and hence assessment of the match at our accommodation near Lake

> Hume, about twenty minutes outside of Albury. Where are Elon and his satellites when you need them? I saw us take the lead from a Sonny penalty, and then an equaliser, before the wheel of death kicked in. By the time I recovered the signal, we were two one up, that man Johnson having done it again. In what was an open and entertaining match, we had the better chances and should have put the game to bed, before the inevitable late push by Roma led to an equaliser in added time. Probably not a disaster, but we need to start winning again in this competition.

If you're wondering what a middle-aged stag weekend in Albury-Wodonga looks like, it comprises fishing, barefoot bowls, karaoke, golf, poker, an 80s band and lots of beer. Beyond that, as they've not previously been known to say around those parts, what happens in Albury-Wodonga stays in Albury-Wodonga…

CHAPTER 5

December 2024: Are You Not Entertained?

After the Lord Mayor's Show...

(idiomatic) Said of a disappointing or mundane event occurring straight after an exciting, magnificent, or triumphal event.

Following the stag and hen weekends, Tracy and I had one night in Sydney, which coincided with the Fulham game. With the intention of watching the match back at the home of Sydney OzSpurs, the Surry Hills Hotel, we booked a room at the hotel next door, 202 Elizabeth.

The reason we stayed at 202 Elizabeth, and not the Surry Hills Hotel itself, is because the latter is not actually a hotel. There was a time in Australia when an establishment could bypass liquor laws if they offered accommodation. Many pubs were therefore called hotels, even though they had few rooms available, sometimes only one. Over the years, with the law becoming a distant memory, many of these hotels stopped the pretense of offering rooms, but the word 'hotel' has remained synonymous with 'pub'. The Surry Hills Hotel would undoubtedly have been one such establishment, although it has had many names throughout its history. Curiously, I have discovered that its first name, when it was opened in the 1840s, was The Cheddar Cheese Hotel. Can you believe it? The home of the Sydney OzSpurs was the original cheese room! I must tell the podders.

Kickoff was at half past midnight. It became very clear, about two hours before the allotted time, that following two big nights out on a stag weekend, and a seven-hour minibus journey back to Sydney, a third consecutive night staying up into the early hours was not going to happen. I would have struggled with it when I was 18, but at 59 it was a definite non-starter. The 40 inch television at the end of our bed offered both screen-sharing with my mobile devices and the option of watching the match after nine hours of sleep. It was too alluring a proposition to ignore.

Monday, 2 December 2024. 202 Elizabeth, Sydney, NSW.

Premier League: Tottenham Hotspur 1 Fulham 1

This was definitely not a match to stay up for and watch live in the pub, post-stag exhaustion or not. A late withdrawal of Solanke with illness, combined with Ange's decision to rest Kulusevski, left us with a front line of Werner/Son/Johnson. The back line also remained weakened without the injured Romero and VDV. From the outset, the game looked very even and soon Fulham started to look the better team, exploiting the space behind our wing backs with pace. Early in the second half, we took the lead against the run of play with another neat finish by 'goal machine' Johnson, his tenth of the season. The man is becoming something of an enigma; his general play is not particularly impressive, but he scores a goal every two games. A deserved Fulham equaliser followed, as it always looked like it would, with a shot from the edge of the box by Cairney. Kulusevski was introduced to save the day and had an impact when the Fulham goal scorer raked his studs down the back of the Swede's calf, VAR prompted the referee to take another look, and a red card was produced. Despite the man advantage, the game ended in a draw, something of a relief after what had happened against

Ipswich in the previous home game. This match clearly demonstrated that we didn't have the strength in depth to be able to cope with multiple injuries, with fixtures coming thick and fast.

After a good night's sleep and watching the Fulham game in bed, we checked out and embarked on the next leg of our travels. This time, our vehicle of choice was not Winston but Mae, the nickname given to our Maserati GranCabrio Sports car. At this point, you'll be thinking one of two things: 'wow, they have a Maserati, that's cool', or, probably more likely, 'flash bastards!' Can I sway you by telling you that the number plates read COYS1? It is debatable which is the biggest waste of money, the car or the plates. In Australia you don't own the plates, as you do in the UK, you lease them from the State Government by way of an increased annual registration fee. I justify this by seeing it as a voluntary additional tax, which I trust will be spent on useful things, like hospitals and schools.

Heading south out of Sydney down the coast, the first stop on our road trip in Mae was Jervis Bay. As you will recall, this is the location of the Federal Government's own little piece of coastline, Jervis Bay Territory (JBT). Naturally, we needed to check it out whilst in the area. To access JBT, you have to pay $20, the Federal Government having come up with the ruse of making the whole place a national park, so they can charge you to get in. For this princely sum, you get access to three roads and a few dirt tracks. The three roads take you to a botanical garden, a lighthouse and a boat ramp, respectively. There are also two small villages, one being a restricted access aboriginal settlement and the other being both the administrative centre of the Territory, a small office building, and HMAS Creswell, a naval base.

On the day we parted with our $20, the roads to the botanical gardens and the lighthouse were closed, meaning for our money we visited a small boat ramp and possibly the least impressive beach on the east coast of Australia. I couldn't help feeling that the whole thing was a microcosm of the Federal Government's modus operandi; overcharging for the privilege of receiving very little in return, and spending the money on naval infrastructure.

In a double Premier League week, the midweek game took us to Bournemouth, a club I have a soft spot for. As a young lad, I used to visit my grandfather in Mudeford, near Christchurch, and occasionally go to a game at Dean Court, the home of AFC Bournemouth. They were in the Fourth Division then. Since that time they have had an extremely chequered history, going into administration twice and suffering multiple points deductions. Finally, some stability broke out, courtesy of a consortium of savvy local businessmen, and Eddie Howe took them from League 1 to the Championship in 2013, and up to the Premier League in 2015. I'm happy to see them now consolidated as a top tier club and doing so well. Only just not this week...

Friday, 6 December 2024. Mallacoota, Victoria.

Premier League: Bournemouth 1 Tottenham Hotspur 0

That didn't go well. Adopting a rotation policy to protect key players, Ange left Sonny and Porro out of the starting line-up. Solanke was back from illness and Gray stepped into the right back position. We started brightly enough until, about 15 minutes in, we decided to leave Bournemouth's beanpole-like centre half completely unmarked at a corner. The young man couldn't believe his luck, heading past Forster unopposed. We huffed and puffed a lot for the remainder of the match, but never looked remotely like blowing the house down. In fact, we created no chances of any substance at all, generating a measly xG (expected goals from chances created) of 0.58. We looked vulnerable on the break and only some profligate finishing from the home team, who amassed an xG of 3.31, and should therefore have scored 3, left the scoreline unchanged through to the final whistle. This was not an Angeball style defeat, where we went all out in a high-intensity attack and were hit on the break. It was just plain old pedestrian football, against a better team.

Like pretty much every Spurs fan whose opinion I encountered, I was really disappointed with the football we played this week. It's not that the Ange magic is not working, it's not been in evidence at all. Have the players lost faith in the system? Is it too hard for them to keep playing with intensity whilst we have two games per week? Or, worst of all, has Ange been rumbled? His doubters claim that his style of football may work in lesser leagues, but he will be found out in the EPL. Could they be right? Am I a fool? I guess I've backed this (blinkered) horse and I'm going to have to stick with it. Am I having doubts? Hell, yes. It's clear we are performing like a mid-table team, much like The Cheese Room's Seb Short predicted after the Woolwich defeat. The Premier League seems way beyond us already. A European berth, and probably a minor one, is all we can hope for. Surely, though, we can pull it together for the cup competitions. I resolve to make that my primary focus. We're still in the rebuilding phase. The league was never a realistic proposition. But Ange wins trophies in his second season… we can beat anyone on our day… we are still in three cup competitions… in Ange we trust!

As you can see, I have put my faith in the power of positive thinking. It's about all I have to work with, at least until the Chelsea fixture.

Road Trip Blues.

One of Tracy's claims to fame is that she hit a kangaroo in the Maserati. Kangaroos being hit by vehicles is an extremely common occurrence in regional parts of Australia. They have no road sense whatsoever. The key to surviving coming together with a kangaroo at speed is to have either a big powerful four-wheel drive with kangaroo bars across the front, or a low wedge-shaped car. In the former case, the kangaroo simply bounces off the front of the vehicle, in the latter the unsuspecting marsupial is scooped up and shovelled off to the side. This is in fact why Mae has such a low front. She was designed to deal with errant kangaroos.

There are a number of reasons why having a Maserati sports car in Australia doesn't make any sense whatsoever, despite their kangaroo handling qualities. One is the cost, another is the condition of the roads, and the third is the speed limit. In most states, the maximum speed you can drive at is 110 km/h. If Mae were to be driven at just half of her maximum speed, she would be 20 km/h over this. Of course I always stick to the speed limit, it would be reckless not to! What is fun, though, is that I can ignore all those 'advisory' speed limits that the authorities provide at every bend in the road to encourage me to slow down to take the corner. I just stay at the same speed, turn the steering wheel, and she sticks to the road beautifully.

By the time the Chelsea game took place, we had arrived on Phillip Island, a popular holiday destination, not far from Melbourne. The place is synonymous with motor racing. This began in 1928 with the 100 Miles Road Race, Australia's first Grand Prix, run on public roads. In 1956 a permanent circuit opened. Mae would have loved to have had a spin. If we'd realised in advance, we could have timed our visit to coincide with one of their track day drive events. We've been meaning to take her onto a race track ever since we bought her, although I know I wouldn't have the nerve to push her to the limits. Tracy would be far better at it than me.

Monday, 9th December 2024. Phillip Island, Victoria.

Premier League: Tottenham Hotspur 3 Chelsea 4

Despite the surprise return from injury of both Romero and VDV, we lost again. Not helped by the fact that both failed to complete the match. At least this time we gave Angeball a go. The early high tempo press had a particularly deleterious effect on Chelsea full back Cucurella, who appeared to have taken to the field in a pair of ballet shoes. Two slips in the first 15 minutes led to early goals from Solanke and Kulusevski. The two goal lead was to be short-lived and from the point Chelsea scored, with Cucu now unhelpfully (for us) wearing a pair of football boots, they looked the better team. We may have got something from the game had our two key holding midfielders, Bissouma and Sarr, not both given away needless penalties. A goal from Sonny after good work from substitute Maddison brought the difference back to one, but it was too little, too late.

For our return journey to Sydney, we took an inland route, to make the whole trip a big loop. This included a night in Wagga Wagga. In aboriginal languages, repeating a word indicates a plural, or 'many of', which makes sense when you think about it. There is some conjecture about whether the word Wagga derives from the Wiradjuri for crow or dance. So the town is either named after many crows or a lot of dancing. Or, possibly, a dancing crow. We were surprised at what a beautiful city it is, seemingly having had more than its fair share of state funding.

I'm sure this would have had nothing to do with the infamous secret relationship between the former State Member of Parliament and the former Premier of New South Wales. Acting out his city's name by crowing in the ear of the Premier, not to mention partaking in a bit of horizontal dancing, was certainly a novel way of benefiting his constituency. For those not familiar with the story, the clandestine relationship ended both of their political careers.

The Rangers match took place on Friday 13th. If you hadn't worked it out by now, the dates of the matches stated are in the time zone of my location at the time. In Australia, the matches often take place on the date following the one it was actually played on in the UK. This always being the case for evening kick-offs, and mostly the case for daytime matches too. Would Friday 13th prove to be another Spurs horror show for the loyal Australian supporters, we wondered...?

Friday, 13th December 2024. Goulburn, NSW.

Europa League: Rangers 1 Tottenham Hotspur 1

With Davies having also joined the injury list, our centre back line-up was down to bare bones, Dragusin being partnered by the versatile (but still only 18 years old) Archie Gray. Bentancur was able to play in the Europa League whilst remaining banned from the EPL. It seems the Europeans were not as offended by his racism as the English. Kulusevski was rested, giving Werner an opportunity to start.

None of these changes worked well. Gray tried to do a VDV and dribble up the pitch, getting caught out on multiple occasions. Bentancur was largely anonymous, and Werner captured the headlines when he was hooked at half-time and replaced with Kulusevski. Ange later publicly labelled his contribution as "not acceptable." In an error laden game, Rangers looked the more likely to score for the first hour, which they eventually did. A clearly unimpressed Ange brought on Bergvall, Sarr and Solanke. The personnel changes wrested back control of the game, resulting in an equaliser, coolly taken by Kulusevski. An honourable mention goes to Bergvall, who played his best football to date in a Spurs shirt.

So this turned out not to be the latest in the Friday the 13th horror franchise, but it certainly wasn't Love Actually either. As I commented on the Cheese Room patreon chat, "We're a bang average team at the moment. Not going to win anything unless there's a really big turn around." It's all getting monotonously depressing. But we're playing Southampton at the weekend. With Saints holding up the rest of the Premier League (I was going to say rooted to the bottom of the table, but you can't say that in Australia), this is surely a match Spurs will win…

A Full Moon, and Lots of Sun

By the time of the Southampton match, we had deposited Mae back with the dealer for safekeeping and returned to Gilgandra Caravan Park. In our absence, this had been the scene of a disturbing incident the previous week. We have a boom gate at the entrance, which we installed to stop customers from coming into the park after closing time, and there is a CCTV camera which allows us to see when vehicles are entering. One evening last week a couple arrived at 7.15pm, well after our closing time of 6.00pm. For reasons best known to her, the female decided to walk up to the camera, drop her trousers and present her fulsome derriere. Not a cheeky little flash, but a full-blown moon. I imagine her and her partner thought this was funny. At first reading you might think so too. But bear in mind that our two young grandchildren are often in the office and can see the CCTV screens. This was a case of indecent exposure.

It might have been left at that had a policeman not popped in the following day to book a cabin for the forthcoming emergency services Christmas party. When he was shown the footage, he took it most seriously, noting that there is a children's play area adjacent to the camera. He saw it as a case of indecent exposure *at a children's playground*. We will have to see how this situation pans out. If only the camera had done just that, we might all have been spared a sight we would rather not have witnessed.

I have more of an affinity with Southampton than most other English Premier League opponents. They are a typical community minded smaller city club who don't offend anyone. Other than Portsmouth fans, that is, to whom they are 'scum'. Spurs often struggle to do as well as they should at Southampton, the 4-0 FA cup loss of 2003 being one example. One iconic night at the old Dell did lead to a famous Spurs win, however, in what supporters of a certain vintage will recall as 'the Ronnie Rosenthal night'. In an FA Cup Fifth Round replay, Spurs were two down on 60 minutes when then manager Gerry Francis turned to Rosenthal to come off the bench and lead the line. Ronnie's left boot contributed the two goals that took the game to extra time, and then a third for his hat-trick, as Spurs ran away with it 6-2 at the end of the additional half hour. Ronnie's achievements that night are remembered fondly, partly because they were so unexpected. In 100 games for Spurs as a forward, he scored just 11 times, 3 of them on that one memorable night in Southampton.

I usually get up and watch the match straight away, but in the morning after the Southampton game I did my six kilometre run first. At 7.45am it was already 24C, and the mercury was due to hit 38C in Gilgandra later in the day. It was a strange feeling, running the streets knowing the game was finished, but not knowing what had happened. As I ran, I speculated that a defeat in this game and I wouldn't be the only Australian feeling the heat…

Monday, 16th December 2024. Gilgandra Caravan Park, NSW.

Premier League: Southampton 0 Tottenham Hotspur 5

With Ange still rotating players despite the injury crisis, Porro was left on the bench to make way for a debut start for Djed Spence. There's been mystery surrounding Spence ever since he was signed, only heightened when he was recently given a new contract, despite being unwanted by Conte and seemingly unfancied by Ange. As if to prove everyone wrong, he assisted a goal for Maddison in the first minute and went on to put in a thoroughly decent performance. With Udogie going off injured, bringing a sudden end to Porro's night off, we might be seeing a fair bit more of Spence in the coming weeks.

Against an abject Southampton defence, we were three up within a quarter of an hour and five up at half-time whereupon, in cricket parlance, we declared. The second half became an exercise in energy conservation, injury avoidance and a chance to give some youngsters a run out. Against such a weak opponent, it's difficult to take too much out of this game, other than that it was a timely confidence boost after recent results. The Spurs supporters entertained themselves with a new song: "I don't care about Levy, he don't care about me, all I care about is Kulusevski." This was good news for Ange, with the supporters on his side and anti-Levy. It surely makes his position more secure. Not something that could be said for the Saints manager, Russell Martin, who was sacked before the night was out. As Ange observed, the 'sacked in the morning' chant is going to have to be revised.

So Ange avoided the heat, even if Daniel Levy didn't. In Gilgandra, meanwhile, the sun bore down on us and the heat wave went on.

Whenever Tracy is asked why she moved from the UK to Australia, she simply replies, "It was raining." Following a particularly wet late summer in 2008, during which the sky remained grey and regularly gave up its precipitation, she took up an offer of a one year maternity cover role in Sydney, from which she never moved back. Not only does Tracy dislike the rain, she loves the sun. In Gilgandra, and mostly in Sydney, the prevailing condition is blue sky and sunshine. What many don't realise is that the annual rainfall in Sydney is more than Manchester, it's just that it literally never rains, but it pours.

What's more important is not the weather on any one day but the climate throughout the year. And so it is with football teams. Until recently, the climate at Manchester City was like Abu Dhabi, sunny all the time. Ironic, given where the funds for the (alleged) 115 counts of cheating originated. It's been hot, it's been predictable, and rain was rare. Happily for the rest of us, there's been a localised outbreak of climate change over the Etihad Stadium this season. The other leading clubs, currently Liverpool and Woolwich Wanderers, have climates like Sydney. Mostly it is sunny. Occasionally there's a downpour, but soon enough the sun is out again.

There's a saying that describes the climate in Melbourne, where Ange grew up, 'four seasons in one day.' It describes the current Spurs climate perfectly. There is no knowing what will happen on any one day.

Later in the week Manchester United were the visitors in the quarter final of the Carabao Cup. An important game in Spurs quest for some sort of trophy this season. We were pretty much guaranteed sunshine in Regional NSW, as the heat wave continued, but what would the proverbial football climes bring to the Tottenham High Road on a Thursday evening in late December?

> **Friday, 20th December 2024. Gilgandra Caravan Park, NSW.**
>
> **Carabao Cup: Tottenham Hotspur 4 Manchester Utd 3**
>
> Phew, that really did turn into a Melbourne kind of day!
>
> I'd become used to the makeshift look of the team, particularly in defence, with the Dragusin/Gray pairing growing in confidence

game by game. Spence earned himself another start, following his impressive display at Southampton, and Bissouma came back in place of Bergvall, following a one match suspension.

In the first half, conditions were fair and the game evenly contested, with Spurs going in 1–0 up following a sharp finish from a rebound by Solanke. Early in the second half, the proverbial sun came out and shone brightly as we scored twice, through Kulusevski, and a second from Solanke. Alas, storm clouds arose when Fraser Forster got into the Christmas spirit early and gifted United two goals courtesy of catastrophic mistakes with the ball at his feet. Rain clouds persisted for an uneasy final quarter of the match, before parting for a moment of blue sky as Sonny scored directly from a corner, with two minutes on the clock. A brief final shower saw United net from a corner but, to the immense relief of the faithful, that was the end of a chaotic second half.

"Are you not entertained?" quipped Ange in the post-match interview. That would be one word for it. Emotionally drained would be two more.

This was a week in which the fun returned to supporting Spurs. Nine goals in two matches, both victories. I was happy to see Ange in top form and enjoying his work despite the adversity of the injury crisis. His belief is that these challenging times will bear fruit when we hit clearer waters with first team players returning from injury in the new year.

We drew Liverpool in the Carabao Cup two legged semi-finals to be played after Christmas but, before that, we host them in the EPL next weekend. The bookies have Liverpool as firm favourites, but my optimism is back and I reckon we can upset them. Our record against teams from the North West so far this season reads: played 5, won 5. Bring on The Reds.

That's Entertainment

'The Jam' was my favourite band when I was young. The words to their seminal song 'That's Entertainment' captured the mood of the nation as the UK struggled through the 1970s and into the 1980s. Power cuts, the three-day week and garbage on the streets in the seventies led into a recession, and riots in the North of England in 1981. Racial tensions simmered on, becoming the catalyst for the 1985 Broadwater Farm riots in Tottenham.

It was not just Ange's 'are you not entertained' comment that brought this song to mind. Last week Tottenham Hotspur announced a partnership with Netflix to promote the new series of the Korean thriller series *Squid Game*. The deal included 'experiential activity for fans, with the infamous *Squid Game* guards roaming the stadium in their pink hooded jumpsuits for photo opportunities and a giant blimp of the Young-hee doll – featured in the 'Red Light, Green Light' game – appearing outside the stadium pre-match'. It's been widely reported that this is just one of a series of planned collaborations with Netflix. In the same week, it was announced that 50 Cent and Mary J Blige will be appearing at the stadium in July.

Undoubtedly, the quality and variety of entertainment on offer to the public has improved since The Jam's idea of a good time was 'lights going out and a kick in the balls'. Daniel Levy's strategy is to leverage this wider entertainment market and, as described in the *Squid Game* press release, 'place the club at the centre of popular culture'. Increasing revenues in this way is within the Premier League's financial sustainability rules. Levy would argue that these initiatives will help fund the acquisition of players, and hence flow through to success on the pitch.

There are a couple of problems with this strategy. The first is that much of the fanbase hates it. They think initiatives like the *Squid Game* collaboration make Tottenham Hotspur a laughing stock and undermine its credibility as a serious football club. The presumption that the supporters would want to see their club 'at the centre of popular culture', let alone actors mingling with the crowd dressed in pink hooded jumpsuits, feeds the cynicism and reveals an agenda at the heart of the club far removed from that of the supporters. I understand that view. It was my gut reaction when I saw the press release too.

The other problem with the strategy is that there is little evidence of it working, or even showing any signs of working. I believe the supporters wouldn't give two hoots about the club becoming a broad based entertainment business if it was accompanied by success on the pitch. The longer the strategy is pursued with increasingly bizarre 'revenue opportunities' failing to deliver any tangible benefit to the team, the more the pressure on Levy will grow.

Meanwhile, the football on display at the stadium has started to look like a parody of the entertainment culture that the club aspires to. Following the seven goal Carabao Cup extravaganza, the Yuong-hee doll and pink hooded actors were treated to an even more bizarre goal fest against the Premier League leaders.

Monday, 23rd December 2024. Gilgandra Caravan Park, NSW.

Premier League: Tottenham Hotspur 3 Liverpool 6

It quickly became evident that my newly rediscovered sense of optimism was not going to survive the visit of Liverpool. With limited options available to him, Ange put out the same team that had started the previous Thursday. Liverpool had played a day earlier in their Carabao Cup quarter-final and were able to rest half the team. From the outset, the evident freshness and undoubted quality and confidence of the visitors put us on the back foot. Liverpool squandered a few early chances, but it was no surprise when they soon moved into a two goal lead. A goal against the run of play from Maddison never really provided any prospect of a recovery and on the stroke of half-time we conceded again to go in 1–3 down.

Whilst in the first half we made a reasonable show of trying to outplay the best team in the league, and failing, in the second half we just looked naïve. Continuing to push forward at every opportunity, we regularly lost the ball and each time we did, the transition of play translated into a break from which Liverpool looked like scoring. Twice, they did. At 1–5 down, our game really kicked into gear and we won the remainder of the match 2–1!

At 2–5, the crowd sang Ange's name. It was all a bit bizarre.

Maybe there's something in this entertainment argument. One article I read this week made a very strong case for football being all about having fun. Only a very small number of clubs actually win a trophy any one year, and most hardly ever. It doesn't stop them from attracting millions of supporters. Football must be about more than just the pursuit of success. Another article this week, by Jack Pitt-Brooke, Tottenham Hotspur correspondent for The Athletic, focussed on the rise of support for the club in the United States. Many local supporters, he suggested, are attracted to Tottenham Hotspur because they are the underdogs. They buy into the dream of someday success arriving, and being all the sweeter for the wait.

Fun isn't the right word, though. As Ange says, it's also about suffering. Football gives supporters the opportunity to feel something every week. What Angeball does is heighten those feelings. In the past, he has been able to combine those heightened feelings with success on the pitch. The Holy Grail! He might do that at Spurs. He might not. Either way, the experience will have been more entertaining than what went before it, and we should be grateful for that.

For me, as a child, football at this time of year was always an exciting occasion, particularly when we were at home and it provided an excuse to get out of the house into the cold winter air. Sadly, only one Christmas match sticks out in my memory, and for all the wrong reasons. It was 23rd December 1978, against the old enemy. All the talk in the playground at the time was whether Glenn Hoddle was better than Graham Rix. Whilst the history books show who won that particular argument, it was a diminutive Irishman that won the day. A Liam Brady masterclass saw us defeated 0–5 by them from up the road. I mention this partly to exorcise a distant but still painful memory, but also as a reminder that the current state of affairs at least isn't as bad as that day.

Spending Christmas at the caravan park is a far cry from the seventies, when I worried about whether the match was going to be postponed due to snow. Now I worry about heat waves and sunscreen. On Boxing Day, it's become a tradition to fire up the outdoor television on the side of Winston to watch the Melbourne test match. With the Apple Box duly relocated to facilitate this, my sports viewing arena temporarily moved to the open air, where a thunderstorm was raging at 2am, kick-off time at the Stadium. It was still windy, but dry, by the time I got out of bed to watch the match.

Friday, 27th December 2024. Gilgandra Caravan Park, NSW.

Premier League: Nottingham Forest 1 Tottenham Hotspur 0

Well, that wasn't entertaining. I felt like I had seen this game before, a 1–0 loss away. The same as at Palace, and at Bournemouth. The formula to beat us seems pretty clear now. Let us have the ball, defend deep and in numbers, hit us on the break once. Job done.

> Bentancur was back after his suspension and Johnson came in to see what he could do at his old club. Kulusevski went into midfield and Maddison dropped out. Fired by the reaction from his former supporters, Johnson looked like he was trying extra hard to make an impact, but largely failed. Once again, we saw a lot of huffing and puffing but very few chances created. With Dragusin going off injured and Spence picking up a second yellow late in the game, we may not have a defence for the visit of Wolves in three days' time.

The repetition of these miserable performances is starting to wear thin. Emotionally, I'm starting to feel drained. Having the opportunity to feel something every week is fine, I'd just prefer it if that thing could be happiness a bit more often. I'm trying to stay optimistic, and keep faith that things will improve, but there's little sign of it. It's not like a five goal loss to Woolwich, but it's depressing, nonetheless. Thank goodness there's some more positive news to report. This week my daughter Anna became engaged to her partner Ben, a fine young man who we have come to know and love. We have a wedding to look forward to in 2026! Meanwhile, there's one more match this calendar year and we're into 2025, the year I've predicted the trophy drought will end. Things need to turn around or I'm going to end up publishing a memoir under a false pretence.

A Revelation!

Whilst the prospect of visiting the UK in midwinter was not the most appealing on our travel itinerary, it was important that we went back to see how Tracy's mum Elaine was doing. The dates we chose also gave us the opportunity to catch up with my family for my mum's birthday, on 15th January.

More motivated by finding the best value flights than any desire to be in Greater Manchester for New Year's Eve, we decided to fly on 30th December. A 6am departure time from Sydney International saw me sitting down to watch the Wolves game in the Emirates lounge at 4.00am, shortly after the game had finished at the stadium. This reminded me of another occasion when kick-off was not before, but shortly after, we took off from Sydney, bound for the UK. It was 24th August 2014. I know this because that was the date when Spurs ran out 4–0 winners against QPR. The flight had a live streaming sports channel, allowing me to watch the game in mid-air, somewhere over the Australian desert.

On that same flight, Tracy spotted a misplaced vowel when the captain tried to use his best Queen's English to make an announcement. "Is the captain a Scouser?" Tracy enquired of the cabin steward, a Lebanese gentleman, on whom the word was lost. "Do you think you could just ask him…" Tracy encouraged. A few minutes later, the steward returned and advised us that the captain was indeed a Scouser and would we like to join him on the A380's flight deck after landing? Whereupon we were met by a jolly Everton supporter, if I remember correctly, with the broadest Scouse accent.

"I have to try to disguise it…," he explained with self-deprecating humour, "…don't want the passengers getting nervous and thinking I'm going to nick the radio."

Talking about things being nicked, we've received some positive news in the drama that is the pursuit of DW, Elaine's former carer. Alfie, our man on the case, is a relatively young member of the Greater Manchester Police force. To his credit, whilst his role within the organisation keeps changing, he is determined to retain responsibility for the case and see it through to a successful conclusion. Shortly before Christmas, Alfie reported that the case file had been submitted to the Crown Prosecution Service. We now await news on whether they agree to move forward with a prosecution.

Watching the Wolves game in a semi-comatose state in the airport lounge, and eventually onboard the A380 prior to take off, was a surreal experience. The match itself proved to be yet another disappointment.

Monday, 30th December 2024. Sydney International Airport, NSW.

Premier League: Tottenham Hotspur 2 Wolverhampton Wanderers 2

The game started with an early exchange of goals. As has become customary, the visitors scored first. A neat free kick move produced a shot that beat Forster's despairing dive and went in off the post. Soon after, a powerful Bentancur header from a corner brought us level.

It became clear as the first half wore on that there was little between the two teams. Each was playing a high press and looking to break through the opposition ranks to create an overload on the break. If anything, a rejuvenated Wolves team, inspired by a 'new manager bounce', had more possession. Despite this, we carved out the better chances and should have taken the lead when Johnson was brought down in the box. Sonny, crystallising in the moment a listless overall performance, saw his penalty saved. A late first half goal swept in by Johnson, after a strong run from the ever impressive Kulusevski, put us 2–1 up at the midway point.

Wolves continued to edge control of the midfield in the second half and there was a sense of inevitability about the equaliser, which arrived at 85 minutes. More frustration for the Spurs home crowd. What they had witnessed was again an entertaining game of football, played out by two mid-table teams. And that was really my take-away from the match. We were no better than a mid-table team.

The Wolves game was the halfway point of the season and we'd played every other team in the league once. So a good opportunity to take stock, not only of how the season was going, but of what it had done for my wellbeing. I set out with the intention of committing my full emotional capacity to Spurs, confident that Ange would bring success in the form of a long awaited trophy. I'd endeavoured to watch every minute of every game, and recorded the whole tale for this memoir. How's it going?

Not well, can be the only answer to that question. All the statistics suggest that this season has so far been a backward step. We are losing more games than we win. Ange talks about sticking to the script and playing 'our football', but it's becoming less clear what that actually is. A high defensive line, forwards pressing hard, inverted full backs given licence to attack, it all seems a bit old hat all of a sudden. None of it is a surprise to any of our opponents and most of them have found a way to counter it. The big holes at the back don't help, the absence of our key centre backs accentuating the problem.

Injuries have definitely not helped our cause. The debate around Ange has become whether he can keep his job. Is the injury crisis sufficient reason to justify him maintaining his position which, history suggests, would otherwise be in severe jeopardy? The injuries, that is, in combination with a lack of depth and experience in the squad. Will Levy back Ange with his cheque book when the transfer window opens?

Committing to the emotional journey means opening oneself up to the lows in the hope of experiencing the highs. So far, there's been plenty more of the former than the latter. It's been a painful journey overall, despite some fantastic results. I'm feeling pretty depressed about the whole thing. In my 60th season of following Spurs, I should have known better than to expect anything different.

Despite the undeniable lack of progress, every time I see Ange interviewed, I get a dose of optimism. He doesn't seem flustered, he has confidence in where things are heading. It's what I believe makes him a great leader. I'm sold on his personal qualities. But am I still sold on his footballing acumen? At the moment I have to say... not really. The evidence before my eyes week by week, and as it is encapsulated in the league table, is clear. The football is just not good enough.

Many memoirs tell a story of pain, trauma and suffering, and it appears that this one will be no different. For some, that suffering turns to personal development and leads to a new place, as the story reaches its denouement. A place of enlightenment, contentment, sometimes even joy.

Suddenly, I have a revelation! I see what is happening. The struggles of the first half of the season are a necessary ingredient of this narrative. It was never going to be any other way. The story of the season will be about how persistence and belief turns adversity into triumph, and the glory of silverware, in the second half of the season. I have to keep believing.

CHAPTER 6

January 2025: Diminished Jeopardy

Black and White, and Red All Over

Through the season Tracy and I have followed Spurs over land and sea, as we travel to places that we love. Spoiler alert – Leigh isn't one of them. But it is where Tracy's mum Elaine lives.

Tracy organised a driver to pick us up at Manchester airport and take us to Leigh, 25 km to the west. He was a Leigh native, having grown up in the town. Leaving to live in Ireland at one point, he returned 13 years later because he 'missed the rugby'. By which he meant Rugby League, the most popular sport in these parts, something Leigh has in common with Sydney. Come to think of it, the only thing that Leigh has in common with Sydney. It does have one of the country's finest home and garden centres, Bents, a favourite haunt of Elaine's. Other than that, it's out-of-town retail at its worst. Our driver informed us that the biggest growth of trade in the town centre now features illicit substances. Sadly, the truth of that observation can be seen on the faces of many of the residents.

With the next visitors to the Tottenham Hotspur Stadium being high flying Newcastle, the prospects of a positive result were not looking good. Being in England, I was at least able to watch the game live at a sensible time of day, in the lunchtime television slot.

Saturday, 4th January 2025. Leigh, England.

Premier League: Tottenham Hotspur 1 Newcastle United 2

Five changes from Ange as illness in the camp compounded the injury crisis, including a debut for goalkeeper Brandon Austin.

A controversial Newcastle equaliser quickly cancelled out an early goal from Solanke. As Spurs tried to play out from the back, a pass from the excellent Bergvall hit the hand of one of the Newcastle players, leading to a goal on the counterattack. Ange was furious that handball was not given but in truth it was accidental, the arm was not in an unnatural position, and it was not the goal scorer who handled. All of which means that, by the letter of the law, it's not handball. Newcastle looked the stronger team for the rest of the half and took the lead before the break.

With Dragusin having gone off ill at half-time, our centre back pairing became Gray and Spence, with Reguilon and Porro at full back. Despite this makeshift defensive lineup, the second half turned out to be an unexpectedly good performance from Spurs. Son, Maddison and Bissouma came on to help push for an equaliser, but it never came. Ange said we deserved to win the game. I thought a draw would have been a fair result.

In the aftermath, most commentators remained sympathetic to the challenges Ange is facing and the in/out debate seemed to be swinging towards a consensus of giving him until the end of the season to prove himself. Reassuringly, all the messaging being reported from within the club reinforced a commitment to the project.

Meanwhile, poor Brandon Austin, having waited ten years for his first chance to start for the first team and putting in a decent performance, came off the pitch to discover that we had made our first signing of the January transfer window. Antonin Kinsky, the Czech international goalkeeper. Thanks Brandon, back to the bench, mate.

It snowed this week, so our ability to get out and about with Elaine in her wheelchair was severely limited. Normally, when we spend time with Elaine, and it's not so cold, we get out into the countryside. We'll visit one of the many stately homes and country estates that are the legacy of the enormous wealth created during the industrial revolution. These properties show how wealth was highly concentrated in relatively few people, with a vast gap between the wealthiest and most of the rest of the population. Something we would not see if there was a similar revolution today, say a digital one. Oh, no, hang on a minute…

Later in the week, the highlights of my sports streaming extravaganza were the first legs of the Carabao Cup semi-finals. After a most enjoyable evening watching Woolwich lose to Newcastle, attention turned the following night to our fixture. Suffice to say, I was pinning my hopes on the FA Cup and Europa League to fulfil my trophy prediction as we headed into this semi. The chances of beating Liverpool over two legs seemed slim.

Wednesday, 8th January 2025. Leigh, England.

Carabao Cup: Tottenham Hotspur 1 Liverpool 0

Yes!! Halfway there. What a game this was.

Ange threw the new keeper, 21-year-old Kinsky, straight into the team for his debut and he put in a stellar performance. Assured with the ball at his feet, he showed a great range of distribution. When called upon to do so, he made the saves to protect his clean sheet. At this rate, Vicario is going to have strong competition for his place when he regains fitness.

Some players are almost defined by how good they were when they were young. Manchester United's '17-year-old Norman Whiteside' being a case in point. This year is Norman's 60th season too, coincidentally, but he'll always be 17 in my head. In this game, the other stand out performances were from '18-year-old Archie Gray' and '18-year-old Lucas Bergvall'. Both were brilliant, the latter scoring the winning goal late in the game, following controversy over whether he should have been sent off for a second yellow card. What talent we have emerging in the squad.

This was an excellent performance, and a thoroughly deserved victory. Most noticeable was how well we defended. Without the ball, we quickly took up defensive positions, our full backs less committed than normal to supporting the attack. It appeared to be a clear tactical switch by Ange. We did something similar in the earlier round to beat Manchester City. Does this hint at the tactical tweak that will turn our season around? Or is it just not 'who we are, mate'? Time will tell.

We played well in both matches this week, with contrasting outcomes against the black and white of Newcastle and the red of Liverpool, reminding me of an old joke. What's black and white and red all over? The answer, of course, is a newspaper. But it's not all over. The second leg is four weeks away. I wonder what result the newspapers will be reporting on then. Beating both Manchester teams and Liverpool to get to the final would be an outstanding achievement. The dire performance and near calamity at Coventry seems like a distant memory.

Reflecting on how I feel after recent performances, I am reminded that the fear that comes with emotional engagement is vulnerability. At the beginning of the season, with expectation high, that felt palpable. Now, the inevitability of a mid-table finish in the league has diminished the jeopardy and dulled the senses. In some respects, it's liberating. I can watch the Premier League matches with a slightly detached air of interest. Some are talking about apathy. Ever the optimist, I see it more as the observation of a longer-term plan, as our generational talent emerges over time to become a highly competitive team under Ange's guidance. If he's not sacked in the meantime, that is.

Cup matches offer the sugar fix of a short-term high. That is where I am trusting trophy success will come from this season, and this week has shown how realistic that ambition is. Next up, we ease our way into the FA Cup with a 3rd round visit to non-league Tamworth. Anything other than a win would be unthinkable…

Giants Nearly Slain

For Australians, Tamworth is the third largest inland city in NSW, behind Wagga Wagga and Albury, with a population of about 44,000. It is the country music centre of Australia, on account of its annual Country Music Festival, the second biggest in the world. All of which is admittedly of little relevance to the good people of Tamworth, Staffordshire. Their claim to fame is that the Reliant Robin used to be built there, the three-wheeled car of Trotters Independent Trading Co fame; 'New York, Paris, Peckham'. They also have a non-league football team, for whom a win against a Premier League team would even surpass the humble Robin in their history of achievements.

Winning the FA Cup this year would be massive for us. When I was young, it was for anyone. Over the years, the 'magic of the cup' has slowly been eroded whilst the profiles of the Premier League and the European competitions have grown. Back in 1981 though, as the Chas and Dave cup final song told us, it was 'Ossie's Dream', and it was my dream too. As a 16-year-old, seeing Steve Perryman lift the cup was what I wanted more than anything. And that year Ossie's dream, and mine, came true.

For the semi-final at Hillsborough that season, Dad and I had seats in the front row and I made a banner to drape over the advertising hoarding. In an uncharacteristic burst of creativity, I cut letter stencils out of card and deployed an aerosol can of blue paint onto an old sheet. It read 'Spurs at Wembley 1961-71-81'. I still have it in my collection of Spurs memorabilia, which also contains cup final tickets and programmes from 1981 and 1982. My personal favourite item is the Bristol Rovers programme from 1977, a game Spurs won 9-0, signed by four goal debutant Colin Lee. I accosted him in the Spurs players' car park and asked him to sign it. You could do that sort of thing in those days.

At Hillsborough, nobody noticed my banner amongst the mayhem that ensued around us. There was overcrowding at the Leppings Lane end that day, to the right of us, where most of the Spurs fans were housed. 38 Spurs supporters were injured, including broken arms and legs, and wounds needing stitches. Foreshadowing the tragedy that was to occur eight years later, a turnstile had been opened to relieve pressure outside the ground, and fans without tickets entered. Thankfully, on this occasion, the police opened two perimeter fences and many fans escaped the crush to the pitch side. The failure of the authorities, and in particular the South Yorkshire Police, to learn from the incident and protect the Liverpool supporters led to the devastating catastrophe of 1989. Footage from the 1981 incident was shown at the inquiry into the 1989 tragedy. Nobody should go to watch a football match and never go home. May the 97 Liverpool fans that died in that terrible tragedy rest in eternal peace.

Nine clubs have won the competition since we last did, 34 years ago. This includes all the usual suspects, plus Everton, Wigan, even Portsmouth. For a club like Spurs, who finish in the upper echelons of the

Premier League each year (until this year, that is), even by the laws of probability you would have thought we would have won it at least once in that period.

Curious about the role that good fortune plays in achieving FA Cup success, I looked up the teams we played in our most recent successful campaigns. Actually, not that recent at all: 1981, 1982 and 1991. In both 1981 and 1982, Spurs won the cup without having to play a team higher than 10th in the top division (the First Division, as it was then). In 1991, Spurs won it having drawn teams from outside the top division in every round up to the semi-final. It took one of the most iconic goals in the club's history, a 'that is Schoolboys' Own stuff' free kick from Paul Gascoigne, to see us beat that years' league champions Woolwich Wanderers in the semi-final. We then squeezed past eighth placed Nottingham Forest in the final, after extra time. Unsurprisingly, it really helps to have a favourable series of draws to achieve FA Cup success. Having said that, a list of the teams that have knocked us out in the last few years includes Sheffield United, Norwich City, Middlesbrough, Everton and Crystal Palace. No wonder supporters believe Spurs have not been taking the competition seriously. My hunch is that we won't have that issue this year, with Ange desperate to fulfil his second season trophy prediction.

Sunday, 12th January 2025. Leigh, England.

FA Cup: Tamworth 0 Tottenham Hotspur 3, after extra time.

Whilst playing a team 96 places below us in the league hierarchy should have meant an easy win, we made it anything but.

I am, as you know, a big supporter of Ange, but even I couldn't support his decision to play Werner at centre forward. Not to put too fine a point on it, what the fuck was he thinking? Flanked by Moore on one side and Johnson on the other, this was not a forward line that looked likely to score goals against anyone. And so it proved. Maddison tried to make up for the blunt attack by shooting from range, without success. At the other end, Kinsky looked confident in goal and never really looked like conceding. Nil-all at full-time was, remarkably, a justified scoreline for our part time opponents. To be fair to them, they played out of their skins. They could even have won it in the dying seconds, if they'd converted one of two late chances. The potential embarrassment doesn't bear thinking about.

Before this season Tamworth would have earned themselves a lucrative replay with this result but, sadly for them, the FA changed the rules this season. All games are now decided on the day, through extra time and, if necessary, penalties. Introducing Solanke and Bergvall during the second half had failed to create the goal we needed, prompting Ange to turn to the bench for even more reinforcements for the thirty minutes of extra time. With Sonny, Kulusevski and Spence finally making us look like a Premier League team, a scrappy own goal eventually broke the deadlock in our favour. Kulusevski then put the outcome beyond doubt, before a late third from Johnson gave the scoreline a respectable look (if you ignore the AET acronym in the record books, that is).

In the Carabao Cup, we have played better the stronger our opponents have become. I can only imagine that Ange, with his mysterious line-up for this game, was banking on doing the same in the FA Cup. The draw for the fourth round pits us against Aston Villa away, so this will have to be the case, or we'll be out of the competition before the middle of February. The next round will be only three days after the second leg of the Carabao Cup semi-final at Liverpool. It's going to be a huge week in our season.

The day after the Tamworth game, Tracy and I set off south to visit my parents in the New Forest. It's a beautiful area. I lived there myself for twenty years before emigrating to Australia. It's where my children came into the world. Lying on the South Coast of England, in footballing terms, it separates two Premier League teams – Bournemouth to the west and Southampton to the east. Although by the time anyone reads this, that will most likely no longer be the case. Poor old Saints are on course to be relegated with the lowest points total in Premier League history.

Thinking about the New Forest reminds me of a funny little Blackadder inspired game we play with our grandson, Liam.

"Tell me two things about the old woman," we say. After a few moments of contemplation, Liam tentatively ventures a response.

"She's old... and she's a woman?" Yes! He beams with pride.

I can tell you plenty of things about the New Forest but being new, and a forest, are not two of them. The area was first referred to as the 'Nova Foresta' in the Domesday Book in 1086, which for me makes it pretty old, although I guess maybe not, for a forest. The word forest brings to mind trees, but the New Forest is mainly heathland and enclosed pastures. With the national park being a total area of 566 km2, only about 15% is tree plantations. It used to have more trees than it does now but the demand for wood during various war efforts led to significant felling. I imagine another conversation with Liam.

"Tell me two things about the New Forest".

"It's old, and it's mainly heathland?" Brilliant, lad!

The most engaging feature of the New Forest is the fauna. Ponies are literally everywhere, their road sense only marginally better than that of kangaroos, of which unsurprisingly there are none. There are, however, cattle, donkeys, pigs and deer. It really is wonderful. The main roads through the forest are fenced, but otherwise you take your life, and that of the animals, in your hands, if you choose to speed around the country lanes.

This visit to my parent's New Forest home coincided with Mum's 88th birthday on 15th January. My sister Karen, her three daughters and her four granddaughters all live in the area, so we gathered at a restaurant for a celebratory family meal that evening. It was another occasion on which I was grateful I could access my Australian streaming service and watch a game delayed, because this important family event just happened to coincide with the second North London derby of the season.

Wednesday, 15th January 2025. New Milton, England.

Premier League: Woolwich Wanderers 2 Tottenham Hotspur 1

Suffice to say, the family meal was far more enjoyable than watching the match...

For the first 20 minutes, Woolwich ran us off the park. We were overwhelmed. Dominated. Our midfield of Sarr, Bissouma and Bergvall were completely unable to get a foot on the ball, let alone impart any control over the game. It was thus a complete surprise when we took the lead. Our first shot of the match, from Sonny, took a deflection and crept inside the post. For 15 minutes Spurs supporters enjoyed being in the lead and pretended that we had a chance of winning, despite all the evidence to the contrary. The inevitable Woolwich goal from a corner levelled things up, before a shot across Kinsky brought about his first genuine mistake in a Spurs goalkeeper jersey, sending us into the break 2–1 down.

Ange showed what he thought of Sarr and Bissouma's contributions by replacing them at half-time with Maddison and Johnson. The change improved the balance of the team and gave the second half a slightly more competitive edge, but failed to change the scoreline. This was, overall, another really disappointing performance. The gulf between us and our great rivals looked like men against boys.

Despite my declared liberation from the stress of watching Premier League matches, this one was important for reasons other than the league table. It's a shame the team didn't play as if they felt the same. Ange wasn't able to get them up, even for a North London derby, and afterwards bemoaned the lack of intensity. I wonder if he is starting to doubt himself.

I have always taken the view that watching a game without knowing the result makes the experience more enjoyable, but now I'm questioning that. With so many games ending with a defeat, I'm wondering if it would be better to get the disappointment out of the way quickly, then watch the game at my leisure. Or maybe just the highlights. Or, possibly, not at all. My resolve is waning. I need a pick-me-up win or two next week to reignite the fire.

Running on Fumes

Whilst our winter visit to the UK continued, with Tottenham Hotspur at Everton this week, my mind turned back to Australia. Curiously, both place names can be found not too far from Gilgandra. Tottenham is a small town 137 km away, its claim to fame being that it's the closest to the geographical centre of New South Wales, 41 km to the West. The town describes itself as the 'Soul of the Centre'; a completely meaningless moniker of no real significance. Tommy Silver tried to arrange an OzSpurs weekend there many years ago, but the event didn't come together. In retrospect, that's probably not such a bad thing. Tracy and I have been there, it's... unremarkable. There's another Tottenham in Melbourne. It's an industrial area, recording no population in the most recent census.

On the edge of Gilgandra, there's a small settlement called Everton. It's just 6 km down the road from the caravan park, it's tiny and it has no claim to fame. There is another Everton in Victoria, a small rural town with a population of 203.

All this had me wondering how many EPL team place names I could find in Australia. After some thorough research, I am pleased to share this important information:

Tottenham, NSW, population 263

Everton, Victoria, population 203

Liverpool, NSW, population 247,672 (a suburb of Sydney)

Woolwich, NSW, population 833

Chelsea, Victoria, population 8,347

Manchester, South Australia, population n/a (a 'county' so not a single place)

Aston, Victoria, population 109,705 (an electoral division)

Fulham, South Australia, population 2,920

Brighton, Victoria, population 23,252

Newcastle, NSW, population 508,437 (a city!)

Ipswich, Queensland, population 2,468

Southampton, Western Australia, population 6,253

Not deemed worthy of a place down under: Bournemouth, Nottingham, Brentford, Ham (West or otherwise), Crystal Palace, Leicester, Wolverhampton.

On the day of the Everton match, Tracy and I had lunch at Winchmore Hill Cricket Club in North London. My friendship group "The Lads" formed around our love of cricket and association with WHCC. In the summer at least, it was the centre of my social life, including a joint 18th birthday party there with my great friend Ally. This weekend we had stopped over to see Ally and his wife Lou at their home in St Albans, on our way back up north. By chance, our visit coincided with an important event. Ally's father, Trevor, had been a stalwart member of the cricket club for many years. Following his passing, Ally and his sister Michelle arranged for a new clock to be made for the front of the pavilion in his honour and Ally invited us to attend the unveiling ceremony and lunch.

The timing of the lunch coincided with Spurs' game at Everton. Being in Spurs heartland territory, there were plenty of attendees interested in the game, so it was shown on Sky Sports in the bar. Through careful selection of my seat, I could monitor the first half, whilst enjoying lunch with Ally, Michelle, their families and various non-playing club members.

Sunday, 19th January 2025. Winchmore Hill Cricket Club, London, England.

Premier League: Everton 3 Tottenham Hotspur 2

More injuries sustained in training this week ruled Solanke, Johnson and Bissouma out of the game, leaving an even more threadbare playing roster than previous weeks. Given the players available, Ange changed the structure of the team to a back three, comprising Gray, Dragusin and the returning Davies. Even with my limited viewing capacity, I could see it wasn't working, the back of Spurs' net bulging at regular intervals being an obvious clue. A half-time score line of 3–0 to Everton felt like a catastrophic, potentially even terminal, day in Ange's career playing out in front of our eyes.

With lunch over, I forced myself to move to the bar at the half-time break for a closer look at the impending calamity. Ange wisely threw the towel in on the experimental formation, which steadied the ship and, most probably, brought his position back from the brink. Two late goals briefly raised the prospect of an unlikely and undeserved point. A beautiful chip over several defenders by Kulusevski and a far post tap in by Richarlison from a magnificent cross by Mikey Moore had us praying for a miracle equaliser. But once again, it was too little, too late.

Prior to the next game, our UK winter visit ended and we travelled back to Sydney. On checking our schedule, we discovered that our flight included an unusually long six-hour layover at Dubai, rather than the usual dash from one flight to the next. Tracy spotted a spa just outside the Emirates lounge and announced that she needed a facial and a massage. I politely declined the facial. I'd survived up to then without ever having one and didn't intend to start, but I wasn't going to turn down the opportunity to have a massage. Having availed ourselves of both the shower facilities in the lounge and the expert services of the spa's masseurs, we were lounging in a state of relaxed contentment when Tracy received a very interesting email. Eagerly, she read out a message from Alfie, our man at Greater Manchester Police, advising that the CPS had replied to him with positive news. Subject to some administrative details and a further victim statement, confirming that Elaine had not lent DW the stolen money and jewellery, they considered there to be a very strong case for a prosecution. Tracy immediately messaged Lizzie with the news, eliciting a "FUCK, YEAH!!" message in response. A succinct and heartfelt response that I think we can all agree with.

A brief stopover in Sydney coincided with the welcome return of the Europa League. With two games left in the league stage, we were going to need a couple of victories to be assured of a place in the knockout rounds. Our opponents this week were from the German Bundesliga – TSG Hoffenheim, or, in its full glory "Turn – und Sportgemeinschaft 1899 Hoffenheim e.V." Literally, this translates to "Gymnastics and Sports Community". When football was growing in popularity in Germany, after being imported from Britain during the late nineteenth century, many teams merged with gymnastics clubs, these being the more respectable and established sports clubs in the community. Spurs fans will recall that Jurgen Klinsmann used to pay tribute to this gymnastics heritage by doing a swan dive every time he made it into the penalty box. It drove us mad until he became a Spurs player, at which point it suddenly became a bit of a laugh.

Tottenham Hotspur has no gymnastics in its history but it did used to be known as Tottenham Hotspur Football and Athletic Co Ltd. I know this because that is what it said on the front of my season ticket book back in the 1970s. The reason that the club was so named is not clear, there is no record of athletics having taken place. Companies House online information confirms a company of that name was incorporated in 1898 and still exists today. It's one of 23 companies on the register based at Lilywhite House, 782 Tottenham High Road, of which Daniel Philip Levy is a director. In 2001, when Joe Lewis and Daniel Levy became majority shareholders, via their investment company ENIC International Ltd, just three of the 23 companies registered today existed. Most supporters do not know about the labyrinthine business structure that ENIC has created around the club in the last 24 years. 'Levy Out' may be a simple slogan, but it's a far more complex business proposition.

TSGH, languishing at 15th in the Bundesliga, should be a pushover for the mighty THFC who currently stands (... checks table...) 15th in the Premier League! A real European battle of the giants then, this one.

> **Friday, 24th January, 2025. The Fullerton Hotel, Sydney, NSW.**
>
> **Europa League: TSG Hoffenheim 2 Tottenham Hotspur 3**
>
> The team for this match picked itself. If you were fit, and had anything more than fleeting first team experience, you were in. The bench comprised Mikey Moore, Will Lankshear and a bunch of kids I'd never heard of.
>
> For the first twenty minutes, we played with fluency and flair, creating several good chances and taking two of them; a fine control and strike from Maddison and a rather more fortuitous deflected shot from Sonny. I made the mistake of relaxing, and commented to Tracy that we were playing really well, when the momentum of the play shifted dramatically. All of a sudden, we couldn't keep the ball and Hoffenheim hit their straps. This state of affairs persisted into the second half and the German's pressure finally bore fruit. The match remained on a knife edge for most of the second half before a typical run and shot across the goalkeeper from Sonny brought a third, putting the game to bed. Of course, we conceded again late on and had to endure a nerve-wracking last few minutes, but we got the job done.

It's been a mixed week. Tactically, the Everton match was what in Australia would be called a 'stuff up'. An obvious error by Ange. In light of this, and on the back of what has turned into a disastrous run of Premier League results, I confess I started to check my phone regularly for any news on Ange's position. Well-informed media reports suggested it is secure, for the time being, and 'not being reviewed on a game by game basis'. I feel relieved about that because I'm still hanging on to the hope of a turnaround, to be evidenced by that long awaited trophy.

The Europa League looks to be the most likely trophy to arrive at the stadium this season, and the victory this week was much needed. Ange's team selection showed that collectively the squad is running on fumes. The fit players we have are turning out every 3 or 4 days, even the likes of Gray and Bergvall, who Ange would have expected to ease into first team experience over the course of the season. As it stands, he is fully reliant on them. Paradoxically, the injury crisis is both Ange's biggest challenge and what is keeping him in his job.

The Kids are Alright!

It's funny how people get excited about seeing celebrities going about their everyday lives, but I get it, I do too. Last year, on a flight from Dubai to Manchester, Sir Alex Ferguson was sitting in an aisle seat as I made my way past him wearing a Spurs t-shirt. I could tell he spotted my allegiance by the pitying look on his face.

On our flight to Melbourne, where we were headed to watch the Australian Open (AO), Tracy was in front of me as we proceeded down the aisle, and turned to give me one of those expressions that says 'look who I've just spotted'. At that moment, my eyes fell on an instantly recognisable face. None other than arguably the second greatest batsman in Australian cricket history, and third highest all time test match century maker, Ricky Ponting, or 'Punter' as he is affectionately known. That little buzz of excitement I had whilst being in the presence of greatness was only enhanced by the realisation that I had a wife with such sporting knowledge as to realise the greatness of the man before I pointed him out.

"Did you see her?" she asked as we arrived at our seats. Her? Was this some kind of a joke? "Gladys!' Tracy exclaimed, having spotted the former Premier of New South Wales (of crowing in the ear and horizontal dancing infamy) sat in the same row as Punter! Tracy had no idea of the sporting legend in our midst, who she admitted she wouldn't recognise if she fell over him in the street. I consoled myself that at least I have a wife who can spot a disgraced politician, if not a living legend of the sporting world. The incident prompted a discussion between us about the hierarchy of celebrity status. I suggested that the second greatest batsman in the nation's history definitely outranks a 'here today, gone tomorrow' politician, which Tracy thought was a bit harsh. And I hadn't even mentioned the Independent Commission Against Corruption finding against her!

Last year I wrote a tongue-in-cheek blog post about our first visit to the AO, which I styled as a commentary on Melbourne's global standing. The rivalry between Sydney and Melbourne is fierce on the east coast of Australia, I pointed out. For the rest of the world, the image of Australia is of Sydney; the harbour, the bridge and the Opera House. Melbourne, I pondered, what's the point? Well, we discovered what the point of Melbourne is. And it's tennis. A tennis point! For two weeks each year, the city comes alive, basking in a brief period of global significance.

The size of a tennis court makes the arena compact, compared to a full size (i.e. football) stadium. It feels really intense. The Rod Laver Arena's retractable roof keeps the atmosphere well contained even when open. The matches feel gladiatorial, comprising bursts of action of various lengths, often brief points but sometimes long rallies. As a rally gets longer, the tension ramps up tangibly until a winning shot, or unforced error, releases the energy of 15,000 people. This repeated cycle of tension and release over hours is both exhilarating and exhausting.

Last year's Women's Final was between players from Belarus and China. With both countries led by tyrannical regimes, it was difficult to know which to support. We got behind the Belarusian, Sabalenka, and were rewarded with a victory. This year's Women's Final was between the same Belarusian and an American. With both countries again led by tyrannical regimes, we went with the underdog. 19th seed American

Madison Keys took advantage of some uncharacteristically error laden play by Sabalenka to take her first grand slam victory. In the Men's Final it was less of a geo-political quandary, more one of personal ethics. Italian Sinner lived up to his name with a performance-enhancing drugs charge hanging over him. Not to be outdone, his German opponent Zverev had two domestic violence accusations against him. On balance, the German was perhaps the greatest sinner, but there was no doubt who was the better tennis player. The Italian ran out an easy winner in three sets.

Spurs' next Premier League fixture took place just a few hours after the Men's Final had finished. I had toyed with the idea of joining a Melbourne OzSpurs meet-up to watch the game. With kick-off at 1am, it was in truth a relief when Emma-Jane informed me that no meet-up was planned and I was not letting the side down by heading to bed instead. The lingering impact of jet lag saw me awake early in the morning to watch the Leicester game before breakfast.

Monday, 27th January 2025. The Rendezvous Hotel, Melbourne, Victoria.

Premier League: Tottenham Hotspur 1 Leicester City 2

Another dreadful performance at home to relegation threatened opponents saw us slip closer to being so described ourselves. From the start, there looked to be little between the teams, with players on both sides routinely failing to recognise the colour of their teammates' jerseys and passing directly to the opposition. Sarr was particularly poor in this regard, closely followed by Porro. The latter did partially redeem himself with the cross that allowed Richarlison to nod the ball into the net to give us a 1-0 lead at half-time. After the events of the first game of the season, I was not sucked into any sense of comfort, although the speed of the turnaround at the beginning of the second half was remarkable. With most of the crowd still enjoying their salmon and cream cheese bagel in the salubrious surroundings of the stadium's catering areas, Leicester took advantage of abject defending by Spurs to go 2-1 up. Despite Ange finally contriving a way of allowing Archie Gray to play in his preferred midfield role for most of the second half, and a characteristically bright cameo from Mikey Moore, we never really looked like scoring an equaliser, let alone a turn around for victory.

Next up was the last game in the Europa League stage against Swedish side Elfsborg, against whom we needed a win to guarantee a place in the knockout round of sixteen. I'd somehow booked our car in for a service at the very time that the game took place (our conscience salvaging plug-in hybrid electric SUV that is, not the planet affronting Maserati). Which is how I ended up viewing the match at a cafe in the regional city of Dubbo, 65 km south of Gilgandra.

Friday, 31st January 2025. Dubbo, NSW.

Europa League: Tottenham Hotspur 3 Elfsborg 0

For the first 70 minutes of the match, I wondered what on earth I was going to write about it. Nothing much happened. The highlight was seeing VDV back from injury, eased back into the fray for the first 45 minutes. Spurs had all the possession and passed the ball around confidently, occasionally putting crosses into the box, to be cleared or put out for a corner by the steadfast Elfsborg defence. With Ange keen to protect senior players in the later stages of the match, it was time for some of the kids to come off the bench. And wouldn't you know it, in the immortal words of Roger Daltrey, 'the kids are alright'!

A joyous last 20 minutes saw three excellent goals from the youngsters. First in on the act was Dane Scarlett with a flying header from a superb Kulusevski assist. Next up (...checks phone to be reminded of name...) Damola Ajayi, three minutes into his senior debut, collected the ball on the wing, drifted past two defenders, played a one-two with Scarlett and dispatched the ball into the bottom corner from the edge of the box. Finally, with the last kick of the match, Mikey Moore burst from midfield, wrong-footed a defender, and picked his spot to the right of the keeper. Three excellent goals and a comfortable victory. In all the excitement, I managed to stop myself from crying out, but my arms shooting into the air drew a few concerned glances from my fellow cafe dwellers. The good people of Dubbo seemed oblivious to the significance of events in North London.

Churlish as it seems to besmirch the glory of those last twenty minutes I can't help wondering why we have spent the whole season watching Johnson ($50M) labouring on the wing and, more recently, Richarlison ($60M) charging around like a bull in a china shop, when we have such talent ($0M) sat in the academy.

Despite our form in the cups, the media is focusing on the question of who is most to blame for the disastrous Premier League campaign that is unfolding – Postecoglou or Levy. With the supporters' ire still mainly being vented towards Levy, he's in the lead, although Postecoglou's standing is in rapid decline. Rather excitingly, it turns out that I am going to have to get off the fence and form a coherent view on the matter. Optus Sport has asked OzSpurs to put forward three members to take part in a Fanzone panel discussion and Sydney OzSpurs leader Nathan has asked me if I want to take part. Is the Pope a Catholic?! They've set the date of the filming for 10th February, which is after both the Carabao Cup semi-final second leg at Liverpool and the FA Cup fourth round tie at Villa. The narrative might be quite different by that time, but as things stand, I'm leaning towards #Levyout #Angein.

CHAPTER 7

February 2025: Punditry and Leadership

About Levy

Writing a memoir in real time, not knowing how the story would pan out, seemed like a good idea at the beginning of the season. I was confident Ange would work his magic, and I'd be documenting a glorious campaign. I had the subtitle of the book already worked out in my head 'the year Ange broke the trophy drought!'. Delirious Spurs supporters would flock to obtain my musings, desperate to relive the glorious season. But it would seem that isn't where this story is heading. I admit my pre-season optimism makes me look foolish. But there is a different story emerging and whatever happens from here it will have been a notable season. New potential bylines come to mind: "the end of the ENIC dynasty!" Wishful thinking. "How it all fell apart for Ange," or even, "Relegation!" Hopefully not. I'm still clinging onto hope: "How Ange overcame adversity to break the trophy drought."

I wasn't going to write this book without, at some point, discussing the most powerful man in the recent history of the club. With Levy hitting the headlines because of rising supporter discontent, this feels like as good a time as any. I'll start with some firsthand insight. For the last two and half years of my full-time working career, I had a senior role with Mott MacDonald, a global engineering consultancy based in the UK, and with a fast-growing presence in Australia. It was there that

I came to know a brilliant structural engineer by the name of Spencer Robinson, based in Mott's Brisbane office. Amongst many notable projects, Spencer was a lead structural engineer on the design of the Tottenham Hotspur stadium, before emigrating to Australia where he's now working on projects for the Brisbane 2032 Olympics. During the design process, Spencer met Daniel Levy on several occasions. What he informed me about those encounters were two things in particular. First, Levy likes to be across the details. Not the type of client who sets the brief, appoints the team, delegates, and is not seen again until the ribbon cutting. Quite the opposite.

The second thing, of particular significance to Spencer given his role as structural engineer, was that Levy doesn't like columns. If you're a structural engineer, columns are pretty important. They take the heavy loads from above, in this case the stands, and transmit them to the ground. For Levy that was a mere technicality to be overcome. For him, columns are unsightly, and get in the way of the free movement of people.

"The source of his column-phobia came from White Hart Lane; the back of house office spaces in the old stadium were really congested and claustrophobic. He wanted to ensure the new stadium had maximum flexibility and space," Spencer recalled. The impact of this influence is most clearly seen when viewing the South Stand from behind. What you see are two massive columns supporting the entire structure, fanning out as they rise like giant trees. Populous, the architects, have made a design feature of it and it looks pretty cool. But it wasn't the most efficient structural solution.

A visit to Brentford provided a welcome break from my Levy contemplations, a match for which I had minimal expectations of a positive outcome considering recent performances.

3rd February, 2025. Gilgandra Caravan Park, NSW.

Premier League: Brentford 0 Tottenham Hotspur 2

Defence was the key to this welcome victory. Spence returned to left back, allowing Gray to move alongside Davies in the centre of defence, and VDV to have a few more days to reach full fitness ahead of two big cup matches. Spurs repelled 37 crosses, never looking like conceding and, for a change, looked more likely to score from a corner than concede from one. We have finally caught onto the latest fad of establishing a bout of all-in wrestling around the goalkeeper and whipping a cross into the melee. This tactic resulted in our first goal when one of the Brentford defenders got so caught up in the wrestling that he forgot to watch the ball and scored with his back. 1-0 at half-time.

In the second half, we played a most un-Ange-like low block and soaked up the pressure. Just as it looked like we were going to be celebrating grinding out a 1-0 victory, Sarr put the icing on the cake with a late strike through the goalkeeper's legs. Not a vintage performance, but a much needed confidence boost ahead of a huge week ahead. I refer to two big cup games, not to mention my upcoming punditry debut on Optus Sport.

Levy is undoubtedly a brilliant businessman. I would describe him as visionary. The plan to redevelop the stadium was bold, challenging and a long term undertaking. It took over ten years from announcement to completion. Despite the level of debt taken on to finance the project, the club is in good health financially, because of the tremendous increase in match day revenues, and the many other events that the stadium now hosts. It's a big mortgage, but an affordable one. Levy has overseen all of this, and guided the club into the 'big six' of the Premier League.

We should not take this achievement for granted. Just ask supporters of Leeds United, or Everton.

There may not be a cheese room in the new stadium, but some would say there is an elephant (in the) room. It's where the trophies should be. Many Spurs supporters lay the blame for the trophy drought firmly at Levy's door. The #Levyout brigade claim he has not invested sufficiently in the playing side of the club. They say he has been too involved in football related matters, exerting influence where he should let others lead. There is undoubtedly substance to that argument. If Levy thinks he knows enough about building engineering to influence the structural design of the stadium, he likely thinks he's seen enough football in his days to do the same for the team, both its structure and its components, the players. Undoubtedly Levy has made mistakes, he's admitted so himself. Sacking Pochettino and bringing in Mourinho, then sacking him on the eve of a cup final. Then Nuno, and Conte. We don't know the full details of what goes on behind closed doors to arrive at these decisions, but they appear, shall we say, misguided?

Does the failure of the team to win a trophy for so long reflect a culture for which Levy is responsible? That prioritises commercial interests above the success of the team? The answer has to be yes. He is the omnipotent force within the club. The numbers, measured in (lots of) pounds and (no) trophies, don't lie. Some even claim that Levy doesn't care about winning on the pitch, except to the extent that it translates into income. I understand the frustration, but that's where I draw the line. Levy has been a lifelong supporter. He's dedicated his whole life to the club. He doesn't need any more money. What he needs more than anything, in order to cement his legacy, is for his long-term strategy to translate into trophies. That is why I believe he wants success on the pitch as much as anyone.

The key issue with the #Levyout argument is who would we get in his place? Be careful what you wish for. Do we want to become an arm of the Qatari state, or the plaything of a tech entrepreneur? A sub-division of Netflix maybe, or Amazon? Better the devil we know until a better alternative arrives. With no imminent likelihood of a change in ownership, the only hope is that the owner changes his ways, although Daniel Levy gives the impression of being as unlikely a leopard as you can imagine to change his spots. The first sign of such an unlikely transformation would be not sacking Ange in the current circumstances, which, according to press reports, remains the plan. The other sign would be Levy backing Ange in the transfer market. With two further additions to the squad arriving in the last few days of the transfer window – central defender Kevin Danso from RC Lens, and highly rated forward Mathys Tel from Bayern Munich – maybe there's a glimmer of hope.

Spencer, meanwhile, despite having to deal with Levy's idiosyncrasies whilst designing the structure of the stadium, describes his contribution in glowing terms. "The project wouldn't have happened without him. He's the sort of client Brisbane needs for 2032 – someone with vision and an unrelenting drive to do something awesome," he told me.

The second leg of the Carabao Cup semi-final against Liverpool took place on a momentous day for my 'Australian family', the wedding of Nicky and Graham. With kickoff at 7am our time, the game would not coincide with the event itself. So Tracy and I dragged ourselves out of bed and drove into the City to meet up with the assembled throng of about 40 at the Surry Hills Hotel.

7th February 2025. The Surry Hills Hotel, Sydney, NSW.

Carabao Cup: Liverpool 4(4) Tottenham Hotspur 0(1)

Ange brought the new centre back signing Danso straight into the team, playing alongside Davies, with Gray and Spence as full backs. A Herculean defensive effort was going to be required to overcome Liverpool and take us to Wembley.

Keeping out the best team in Europe needed a flawless performance. It was not to be.

After about half an hour of backs to the wall defending, Bissouma gave the ball away in midfield and it was no surprise when Liverpool capitalised on the mistake for the first goal of the game. All square on aggregate at half-time, and we were still in it, until a mistake by Davies early in the second half again presented our opponents with a gilt-edged opportunity. Inevitably, the chance was taken, and we found ourselves down in the tie for the first time. With nothing to lose, Ange jettisoned his new found defensive tendencies and threw caution to the wind. Richarlison suffered what appeared to be a calf strain and Ange replaced him with our other new signing Tel, playing with great enthusiasm but little end product. Some form of Angeball was attempted, involving Spence playing on the right wing, a fluid three man defence and a high press up front. It was worth a try, but would have needed a healthy dose of luck and a capitulation by Liverpool to have any chance of success. The inevitable result was more rich pickings for the Reds as we over-committed, leading to a 4–0 defeat.

The Sydney OzSpurs disbursed into the morning, disappointed but not surprised by the outcome. Tracy and I at least had a wedding to attend to brighten our day. As we assembled in the sunshine that afternoon, a few fellow guests, aware of my football allegiance, offered their commiserations on the morning's result. In truth, it was soon forgotten. At the beautiful Manly Pavilion on the shoreline of Sydney Harbour, together with our Australian family and many visitors from the UK, we celebrated the love of Nicky and Graham. Dancing like no-one was watching, we sang along with the band until our voices were hoarse, eventually retiring to bed with sore limbs and happy hearts.

Bugger Tottenham Hotspur, who needs them?

'Undeniable'

Attention turned back to the FA Cup this week and I was reminded of what became the greatest experience of my personal fandom.

1981 was the 100th final and, as season ticket holders, Dad and I had the automatic right to buy tickets. We decorated the car with blue and white ribbons and banners, including my handmade effort from the semi-final, and set off for Wembley. Waving and tooting at other similarly decorated vehicles, the sense of excitement and anticipation was palpable as we crawled along the North Circular Road to the Wembley Stadium car park.

The build up to the match involved all the pomp and ceremony of a nationally important event. A marching band, the singing of Abide With Me and the National Anthem. The teams were presented to the dignitaries. Massed ranks of supporters at either end of the old ground swayed and sang in unison, packed onto the terraces so tightly that they appeared to move as one. The match itself was a tense and closely contested affair against Manchester City. At the time, they were a decent team, but nothing like the powerhouse they have become since they became a state-sponsored plaything of the Abu Dhabi sovereign wealth fund. Tommy Hutchinson put City ahead on 30 minutes and, with few chances being created at either end, for most of the rest of the game it looked like that was going to be the end of the scoring. But Tommy's goal-scoring antics weren't over for the day. With a great deal of fortune for us, the hapless sky blue deflected a speculative shot from Glenn Hoddle into his own net to take the game to extra time. My overarching memory of that extra thirty minutes is of players from both sides going to ground with cramp, the fitness levels of players in those days evidently not sufficient to last the full two hours of play.

The following morning I got on my twelve gear Raleigh Record racing bike and took myself down to the Tottenham High Road. The atmosphere around White Hart Lane that morning felt like a continuation of the previous day's celebrations. Spirits were high, particularly amongst the rank-and-file supporters who could not get a ticket for the first game. Tickets for the showpiece final in those days were distributed so widely amongst FA affiliated clubs, FA dignitaries and various other hangers on, that the allocation to each of the participating clubs was only about 20% of the 100,000 stadium capacity. The FA set the date for the replay as the following Thursday which, for the first time in FA Cup history, was to take place at Wembley. For the replay, the allocation of tickets to the participating clubs was far greater than for the first game. With City fans largely unable or unwilling to travel all the way to London for the second time in a week, and on a school night, Spurs fans gratefully snapped up most of the tickets.

That Thursday night will live long in the memory of any Spurs fan in attendance. The atmosphere lacked the ceremony of the Saturday but more than made up for it with the passion of the genuine supporters, singing their hearts out as if they had transported White Hart Lane the twenty kilometres to Wembley Stadium. The highlight of the match was the winning goal by Ricky Villa, an inconsistent player who was capable of great things, as he proved that night. But it wasn't just about that goal. The match was a classic. 1–0 up, 1–2 down, 3–2 up. The sense of euphoria in the Spurs dominated crowd as Steve Perryman went up to collect the trophy was overwhelming. I hugged my dad as the Spurs fans sang 'You'll never walk alone'. At that time, it was a song that was sung widely, not just at Anfield. For a sixteen-year-old, that night was as good as it gets as a Spurs fan. 43 years later, for a 59 year old, that night remains as good as it's got for me. Which is evidence of both the magnifying effect of memories from an exciting time in my youth, and the lack of competing moments since.

FA Cup finals have lost their lustre since the heady days of the eighties but, for Tottenham Hotspur, a win this season would be as meaningful as ever. First, we'd have to overcome a tough trip to Villa.

Monday, 10th February 2025. Manly Pacific Hotel, Manly, NSW.

FA Cup: Aston Villa 2 Tottenham Hotspur 1

There goes another trophy opportunity for the season. One minute into the match, with Porro already defending on the halfway line and Villa exploiting the space down his flank, the first shot of the match seemed to go straight through Kinsky and we were one down. For the next half hour Villa sliced through our midfield at will, images of hot knives and butter coming to mind each time a forward pass caught our midfield out of position. Villa's failure to rack up more goals reflected their abject finishing, rather than any defensive prowess on our part. At the beginning of the second half Spurs came out fired up and full of energy. Ange must have given them one of his famous inspirational team talks. But still we failed to create chances. A second for Villa soon arrived and we never really looked like getting back to parity, despite a very late strike from Tel, topping off what had been an encouraging debut with his first goal for the club.

Straight after the match, it was off to the Optus campus in Macquarie Park to film my first, and probably last, attempt at television punditry. An entire crew of producers, cameramen and our host, former Socceroo, Scott McDonald, greeted me and fellow Sydney OzSpurs Matt Zammit and Rob Anderson. Matt is a former colleague of Tracy's and a really smart guy. It was Tracy's suggestion that he be invited to the show. Rob is a loyal long-standing member of OzSpurs. A goalkeeper himself, he took great delight in wearing the bright yellow Spurs goalkeeper jersey to the filming. He certainly wasn't going to be run over crossing the car park that morning.

The Optus guys were all really friendly and grateful to us for being there, pretending that we were doing them a favour when we all knew what a thrill it was for us to be invited. Scott didn't even seem offended by me not knowing who he was, despite his illustrious career spanning spells at Southampton, Celtic and Middlesbrough. The cameras rolled as we sat around talking about Spurs and trying to look like we knew what we were talking about. I'd learnt a few facts I'd gleaned from the Cheeseheads on the podcast, like the relative spend on salary bills for the top clubs, which I described as a proxy for the quality of the squad. Craig Foster, eat your heart out (or maybe Alan Shearer, if you're British)!

Later in the day, it was exciting to see the programme trending on the Optus app and being shared on YouTube, Instagram and X. Only then did it dawn on me that not only were thousands of people watching, they had a platform to pass judgement on our performance. The feedback was, shall we say, varied?

"These guys are deluded," was one typically acerbic comment.

More positively, "It was good to hear the respondents looking at the situation with level heads. A far cry from so many of the toxic keyboard warriors who can't see the forest through the trees." Thanks for that @doggowhisperer6844, and you received four likes!

My favourite comment was on Instagram. "The guy in the white Spurs shirt is hot!" A shot in the arm there from @mellortracy.

The app and YouTube channel were geolocation restricted, meaning they could only be seen in Australia. Helpfully, Optus Sport also put out an article that summarised the conversation and they used one of my words as the hook.

'Undeniable' – Why some die-hard Tottenham fans are still against sacking Postecoglou.

Andrew conceded to some bias and knows results aren't good enough, but also believes their long trophy drought points to issues beyond the manager.

"My thing with Ange is that my heart is really with him. I really love the guy. He's clearly an excellent leader, an excellent human being, you want him to succeed," Andrew said.

"So my heart says Ange in, my head increasingly looking at the results and what's happening and questioning it. For now, I'm still Ange in, but I don't know.

"There's definitely an Aussie tinge to the support he gets over here, we all want him to succeed because he's one of us right? In the UK, it's very polarised.

"I think most supporters still see his qualities as a person, as a leader of their club, but it's a results-driven business and since the infamous Chelsea game last year which was the end of the good run at the beginning of the season, you look at the results, they've been really poor, poorer than Conte and Mourinho by a long way.

"So a lot of our supporters look at that and just say, 'it's not good enough' and I get that.

"It's the 17th year that we've been looking for a trophy and it's absolutely undeniable that that has to come back to the way the club is being run and the ownership."

Despite all the excitement of my television appearance, in sporting terms this was a disastrous week. The narrative that we were going badly in the Premier League but still in three cup competitions suddenly disappeared. It all now hangs on the Europa League. It's two-thirds of the way through the season and my emotional commitment to the cause is being severely tested. Even my mid-season revelation now looks like a giant clutch at an illusory straw. But I'm going to hang in there through thick and thin. Mainly thin. There's a genre of literature called the survival story and it looks like that could be the section of the bookstore I'm heading to, unless Ange can pull a late Europa rabbit out of the proverbial hat.

Archie "He's that good" Gray

Immediately after my television debut, Tracy and I headed to Sydney airport for a flight to Tasmania. As a Christmas present for Tracy, I bought a four-night stay at Saffire Freycinet, an exclusive hotel on the Freycinet Peninsula, on the east coast of the island. The popular holiday area and national park sits roughly equidistant from the state's two cities, Hobart, the capital to the south, and Launceston to the north. During our time there, Optus Sport continued to slice and dice the video of our Spurs Fanzone discussion, putting more content out on their various social media platforms. One particular four-part Instagram story picked up on a comment I had made about Archie Gray. Having publicly aired my negative impression of Brennan Johnson, who I said was no better than the players coming out of the academy, I focused on Gray as an example of a good purchase.

"That guy will captain England in the future, let alone Tottenham. **He's that good**" was the quote that Optus Sport put on the first page of the story (including the bold font). The next page was a video of me saying those very words, followed by another still frame, this time with an Ange quote about Gray: "I just think he's a fantastic player, I'm just so pleased he's at this football club." The last page was a video of Ange saying those words. They had literally juxtaposed my comments with Ange's, as if they held equal weight! And what is more, over ten thousand people clicked on the little heart icon to show their appreciation for the sentiment.

All of this coverage was becoming compelling viewing, to the extent that Tracy questioned my motives. "You're enjoying all the fame, aren't you?" she teased. I had to admit I was. Although fame is all relative. My flirtation was fleeting, and in fact anonymous, with my quote being ascribed to OzSpurs rather than me personally. The thousands of people who had viewed the content had no idea who I was. Entry level fame, I think you could call that, still well short of doing lines of coke and alcohol fuelled trashing of hotel rooms. That would have been a relief for the Saffire Freycinet management team; the hotel room we were occupying was exquisite, providing breathtaking views of the Hazards Mountains. Never mind trashing it, I felt guilty leaving the hotel staff to make the bed.

It was a fascinating week in which we learnt about Tasmanian devils, oyster farming and, courtesy of the all-inclusive nature of the hotel, the deleterious effects of excessive rich food and fine wine. But the best thing about the week? No Spurs game. Getting straight through to the last 16 of the Europa League meant this was the first week with no midweek match since mid-November. No doubt it was good for the physical health of the players but, together with our week in Tasmania, it was undoubtedly a tonic for my mental health. A gin and tonic, mainly.

Ironically, our next game also involved devils, in the form of Manchester United, the 'Red Devils'. This clash of two of the giants of the game and recognised 'big six' clubs saw 14th placed United pitched against 15th placed Tottenham Hotspur. It was comforting to see that we were not the only big club massively underperforming this season.

Monday, 17th February 2025. Gilgandra Caravan Park, NSW.

Premier League: Tottenham Hotspur 1 Manchester United 0

Five injured players returned for this game. Two started; Vicario and Maddison, whilst three were on the bench; Udogie, Johnson and Odobert. Ange took Archie Gray out of the limelight created by the Optus Sport Instagram post inspired by my quotation. Either that, or he was giving him a rest because he'd played more minutes than any other player in the Premier League in recent months.

United's new manager, Ruben Amorim, had failed to create the fabled 'new manager bounce', in his case creating a 'new manager bellyflop'. His bench was more full of kids than ours had been in recent weeks due to a combination of injuries, suspensions and selling players in the transfer window. He still had a team of well-known players to put out but, in truth, they were terrible.

Spurs started brightly. With the press working effectively and the full backs marauding down the wings, it even looked a bit like the long forgotten Angeball. Spurs' early pressure was rewarded on thirteen minutes when Onana in the United goal parried a shot from Bergvall. With the defenders in red doing an impression of a Madame Tussauds display, Maddison stepped forward to sidefoot the ball into the net. After that, it was a routine display. Both sides missed decent chances, but on balance, the better team won the day. Gray was eventually called into action and there was time enough for Johnson to put in an appearance, and Odobert to remind us what he looks like, before the final whistle sounded.

A welcome second Premier League victory in a row and we've surged up to 12th on the table! With another week of training and recovery unencumbered by a midweek game, and a chance to avenge the home defeat with a visit to lowly Ipswich ahead, things are looking up again. A late recovery in our Premier League form to challenge for a European place is possible, but unlikely. What I'm looking out for now is a sign that with the injured players returning, we can play consistently at a level that might take us all the way in the Europa League. That's a sufficiently exciting prospect to keep me all-in on the Ange bandwagon. The project is still alive.

The week ended with a phone call I received whilst sitting outside Winston at the caravan park. Not recognising the number, I answered tentatively.

"Hello?"

"Andy?"

"Yes."

"It's Steve, from Ozspurs." Now I recognised the distinctive London accent of Steve Palmer. Steve was one of the first OzSpurs members I met at the Surry Hills Hotel all those years ago and I remember he treated me like a friend from the moment we met. Later I realised he does with everybody. But on the phone that day, he didn't sound like his normal chipper self. "Just wanted to let you know the latest about Cam, mate," he said. "It's not looking good, he's in the ICU."

Steve was really worried that Cam would not be with us much longer and was letting a few of Cam's closer friends know. I thanked him and asked him to keep me posted. Cam had been battling cancer for years and I was sorry that I'd not kept in touch with him enough to know how bad things had become. He'd always been good at calling when he received good test results. I should have known not hearing from him meant bad news. Suddenly, my emotional engagement with Tottenham Hotspur felt a lot less important.

On Leadership

This week started with news on our local 'Gilgandra – Living and Social' Facebook page that a plague of locusts had been detected west of Tottenham, NSW. "Medium density nymphs with occasional high densities," was how it was described, which I'm sure isn't as sexy as it sounds. Could this be a portent of impending calamity? An early exit from the Europa League maybe?

I've been thinking about my own leadership journey and how it has informed my opinion of Ange and his approach.

In my first job after graduating, I did all the things you would expect a young building services engineer to do. Working on projects of diverse scale and nature, from schools to office blocks and hospitals, I learned from those around me and gained the skills that made me a competent engineer. But in truth, I never really felt like an engineer, not deep down. Not like some I have met who are engineers to the core; forever tinkering with cars, taking apart household appliances, fixing their neighbour's washing machine for the fun of it. That wasn't me. The mechanics of engineering was just something that I'd learnt how to do. What interested me most was the interdisciplinary nature of building design, particularly when I got to work with great architects.

After ten years of learning and experience, I'd become competent and confident enough to be noticed and a firm called Gifford and Partners headhunted me. I'd come to their notice working on a project refurbishing the offices of Frizzell Insurance in Poole. It's the big building in the middle of a roundabout as you drive there from Bournemouth, for those that know the area. Gifford were the structural engineers, and I was leading the building services engineering. They offered me my first management role. What they had seen in me wasn't a brilliant engineer, but someone with leadership potential.

The role came with a private office at the end of a wing of Carlton House, a former reform school building the practice had converted into its head office on the edge of the New Forest. In the open plan area, immediately next to my office door, sat my personal assistant (the wonderful Angela Ward, who's still a good friend), and then a team of about 20 staff. Fairly soon after my arrival, I realised that not all the team welcomed the new young upstart who had been parachuted into the end office to be their new boss. One by one, they left. It was a traumatic experience, and I was grateful to one of the Partners of the firm, David Dibb-Fuller, who acted as my mentor and re-assured me it would all come good in time. In retrospect, I realised that, for the business, this wholesale change of the team was what they expected from my appointment all along.

As I recruited a new team I became fascinated with the concept and practice of leadership. I decided to hire people who were better engineers than me and create an environment for them that would facilitate their success. I found that better people led to a better reputation, better projects and the opportunity to recruit more good people, and grow the business. It was an upward spiral. My role was to make sure that the spiral kept going in the right direction. It was the approach I employed successfully at Gifford and led to me becoming their youngest ever partner at 35 years of age. It was a wonderful company and I'm grateful that I left when I did, emigrating before the global financial crisis undermined the business model and forced the Partners to sell the business.

I took the leadership philosophy honed at Gifford to Arup in Sydney where, over time, I became both leader of the Buildings Group and Office Leader. During my time in those roles, staff numbers in Sydney grew from 400 to 800, over about five years. It was an exhilarating period. We worked hard and played hard. It's a company with a fantastic brand, a strong underlying set of values and great people. I take pride looking back on those years, not only what we achieved but the fun we had doing it. Next I moved on to Mott Macdonald, another great firm, with leaders that supported me and backed my ambitions for the Built Environment sector, until I jumped off the spiral to lead a new life of travel.

One skill I developed was the ability to plan and articulate a clear vision for what we were trying to achieve. It allowed me to inspire good people to join us on the journey, but also taught me that the relationship between a leader and someone they hire is mutually symbiotic. For the leader: 'I have selected you and am putting my trust in you to succeed because I believe in you. Your success is my success.' For the person being hired: 'You have given me this opportunity and I want to succeed, not only for myself but to repay your trust.' Another leadership attribute I tried to maintain was a values based approach. Doing the right thing, whatever that may be, built trust with those I dealt with and allowed me to sleep soundly at night. Finally, I tried to remain calm and consistent in how I managed situations, which I found gave people confidence in me.

That's not to say that I didn't make mistakes. I made plenty over the years. Just as Ange and the Spurs players have made more of their fair share of mistakes this season. With a visit to Ipswich to test our rekindled league form, hopefully there wouldn't be too many against The Tractor Boys. Despite their position in the relegation zone they're a decent team on their day, as they showed when they came to Tottenham Hotspur Stadium and did us over. It was time for revenge.

Sunday, 23rd February 2025. Gilgandra Caravan Park, NSW.

Premier League: Ipswich Town 1 Tottenham Hotspur 4

A typically spirited Ipswich start gave Spurs a nervous first five minutes, but with Udogie returning from injury on the left, and the in-form Spence moved to the right, the defence held up.

A return to form for Sonny created mayhem down the left-hand side, his brilliance making a fool of the Ipswich right back, as he created two simple chances for Johnson. The enigma they call Brennan put both chances away and can feel happy about his performance, despite making no other significant contribution. A goal against the run of play saw the home side come out for the second half still in touch, but they lacked quality. Spurs' superiority eventually paid dividends with a deflected shot from Spence and a left-footed shot that went in off the post from Kulusevski. A comfortable win in the end, the third in a row in the Premier League and we're building some momentum.

Reflecting on my leadership philosophy reminds me why I am so invested in the success of Ange. He is brilliant at articulating his vision to prospective recruits. He lives his values, and he remains calm and consistent. Ange clearly has some challenges in his role that I didn't. In engineering, I didn't have to deal with staff that regularly became incapacitated, although it happened occasionally. And for nearly all of my career, I had fabulous leaders and mentors that supported what I wanted to achieve. Even if one of them was a Gooner. I feel for Ange in that regard, I'm not sure Levy is the sort of boss I could have related to.

Thursday, 27th February 2025. Gilgandra Caravan Park, NSW.

Premier League: Tottenham Hotspur 0 Manchester City 1

This was a match in which I could apply my theory, that I could watch us play in the Premier League and not be too concerned about the result. I was more interested in the team's momentum, and the strategy Ange was adopting for reintroducing injured players and resting those who had overplayed.

Ange rested Sonny and Kulusevski, which left us with Odobert, Tel and Johnson up front, the weakest frontline since Moore, Werner and Johnson failed to score a single goal in 90 minutes against Tamworth. No wonder we failed to register against Manchester City. After Haaland scored his obligatory goal, City missed a couple of easy chances and we were fortunate to go into the break at 0-1. In the second half, we rallied and with four subtitutes coming on at the hour mark, there was hope that we might get a deserved equaliser. But, yet again, it was too little, too late.

There were a fair number of positives to take from the game despite the defeat. Bentancur looked to be getting back to his best. Bergvall continued to get even better, and there were no more injuries.

There's a week with no game at the weekend, before we see who is available for the round of 16 in the Europa League, where we again play the alphabet extremities, AZ. Will we finally see the return of VDV and/or Romero? We desperately need Solanke back with Tel struggling to make any impact at centre forward. Otherwise, will Ange stick with Tel or put Sonny or even Kulusevski at centre forward? Please, not Timo Werner!

It is clear from the comments Ange has been making in interviews that the Europa League is now the club's target for the season. Looking forward, it feels like we are about to have a mini season within a season; the aim being to fulfil Ange's promise of a trophy in his second season and claim a place in next season's Champions League.

CHAPTER 8

March 2025: A Stay of Execution

Ready to Shine

This week my attention has been drawn back to the subject of gambling by the exploits of a character in this story who I haven't yet introduced. He's a thoroughbred racehorse called Ready to Shine, of whom Tracy and I are proud owners of 5%. There is some conjecture between Tracy and I which 5% we own. I maintain it is his nose, as that's the part that wins the races. And he has won races! Two out of four so far. Which is why I had money in my online betting account at the beginning of the season to bet on Spurs winning a trophy. It was 'free money', acquired through backing Ready to Shine to get his nose over the line first.

Matt Zammit, a friend and former colleague of Tracy's, invited us to join the Ready to Shine ownership consortium. He's an Australian Spurs fan and, you will recall, a fellow pundit on the Optus Sport Fanzone programme. When the horse was acquired, Matt gave the 20 strong ownership cohort the opportunity to suggest, and vote on, a name for the horse. His lineage is from 'Luminescence' and 'Better Than Ready'. My suggestion of 'Luminous Son' was both a nod to his heritage and a tribute to my favourite Spurs player. Sadly, I was runner up, although I confess 'Ready to Shine' does hit the mark.

After his first four races and two glorious victories, Ready to Shine went to have a 'spell', which we have learnt means hanging out in a field. A bit of light exercise, but mainly standing around eating grass. Then, in December, he came back into 'preparation', the period when he is actively training and racing. Apologies to racing enthusiasts if it sounds like I'm teaching grandma to suck eggs. I'm still learning the jargon. It was at this point that Ready to Shine went full Spurs centre back on us and picked up an injury. Our trainer, Matt Smith, is very good at giving us audio and video updates on how the horse is going, but he loves to give positive news. So what we thought was a minor setback turned out to be more akin to a VDV hamstring, or a Romero groin strain, for that matter.

Finally, this week Ready to Shine made it back on track for a trial, which must be a lucky omen for the prospect of either VDV or Romero returning for the Europa League game later in the week. A trial is like a practice race, to make sure he's not forgotten that his job is to run faster than all the other horses and get the 5% owned by Tracy and me over the line in first place. No bets are placed, but you can watch it on the Racing NSW website, as you can the proper races.

Excitedly, we logged in at the designated time to see how our equine investment would fare. Straight away Ready to Shine nestled in close to the rear, biding his time, we imagined, for a late assault on the lead. As the field negotiated the corner, our jockey seemed to be getting little response to his admittedly rather feeble looking encouragement. A push for the line didn't materialise, and it transpired that Ready to Shine hadn't been. Ready, that is, to shine. But Tracy and I, and our 19 fellow investors, had nothing to be concerned about, because trainer Matt reported back later in the week and it was good news! "Really pleased with how Ready to Shine went in the trial," he assured us. "We just wanted to give him a run, not push him too hard and see how he pulled up. He's looking great!"

Consortium lead Matt reported our horse had done his best work "after the finishing line." As you probably realise by now, Tracy and I have very little knowledge about this whole racehorse owning game, but even we know it's better if your horse does its best work before the finishing line. There must be some wider strategy at play here that will reveal itself in due course as Ready to Shine becomes the next Winx and returns us $26 million in prize money. Either that, or he's a donkey.

In possibly the corniest link of the book, I wondered whether the thoroughbreds of the Spurs team would be ready to shine in the Europa League as the next round of the competition got underway in The Netherlands.

Friday, 7th March 2025. Hyde Park Plaza, Sydney, NSW.

Europa League: AZ 1 Tottenham Hotspur 0

The similarities between Ready to Shine's performance in the trial and Spurs' display at AZ were stark. Neither came out of the blocks well. Both were outrun by the opposition and suffered defeats.

Optimism had reared its surprisingly persistent head when the squad was announced and it included Solanke, VDV and Romero. The bubble soon burst, however, when the starting lineup was announced with the trio left on the bench. What is the point in naming them in the squad if they are not fit to play? Solanke did get a run out late in the game, but after falling awkwardly following a fairly innocuous challenge, he limped off the pitch and, presumably, back onto the injury list.

AZ could easily have scored two or three themselves, but in the end settled for the one that we had contributed to their tally. Before this game, Bergvall had only scored once in a Spurs shirt, but not anymore. Attempting to clear a corner, the blond Swede sliced the ball wildly, sending the ball looping over Vicario and

> into the top corner of his own net. What followed was an abject performance from a team that failed to register a shot on target until the 88th minute.

If we're going to keep our season alive, we're going to have to emulate Ready to Shine and do our best work after the final whistle, in the second leg.

Watching this game was probably the most dispirited I have felt all season. This was the start of the second phase. Injured players had returned. Angeball was surely about to be unleashed on the team in 6th place in the Dutch league and we would assert our right to go through to the later stages of this competition. Maybe even win it. But no, we turned out a turgid brand of football, ceded the initiative to the opposition at every opportunity and finished the game as worthy losers.

Sydney

We have rented our Sydney apartment out whilst travelling, so it is a curious consequence of our current sabbatical that when we return to Sydney, we stay in a hotel or Airbnb and experience it like a tourist.

For many years, I was one of the eighteen thousand office workers who commute to work by Sydney ferry, most of them disembarking at Circular Quay as their point of arrival in the Central Business District (CBD). If you've ever experienced the Northern Line on the London Underground at rush hour, this is nothing like that. I mention it because it's the polar opposite. Commuting doesn't get any better than gliding between the Harbour Bridge and the Opera House on a Sydney Harbour ferry.

The ferries are all named after notable Australians. Except when the NSW Government had the idea of holding a public poll to name a new vessel. In a result that perfectly sums up the humour of the good people of the state, not to mention their disdain for the state government, the winning name was 'Ferry McFerryface'. The whole debacle caused a political storm, with accusations of vote rigging and demands for a recount. Before that could take place, Transport Minister Andrew Constance brought some common sense to proceedings and renamed the vessel after a popular children's author, May Gibbs.

Circular Quay's place as the world's primary perspective on Sydney is reinforced by the starring role it plays as the backdrop to the annual New Year's Eve firework display. Six launch barges line up along a six-kilometre axis through the heart of the harbour, from Bradley's Head in the east to Cockatoo Island in the west. The bridge acts as a giant launch gantry. Other launch sites are located atop towers in the city, even sometimes the curves of the Opera House roof. It is a truly spectacular display which for years set the standard globally, before other cities cottoned on and competed, notably Dubai and London. One thing those cities can't do is get in first. Only Auckland and a few Pacific islands could do that. As Australians might say about the prospect of them ever outdoing Sydney... yeah, nah. Which means no.

The image of Sydney witnessed by so many around the world on the last day of the year is a romantic view, but an extremely narrow one. Sydney has many more faces to reveal for those who choose to look.

The geography of Sydney is interesting. With the ocean to the east, it is bound by Pittwater, a large body of water forming the entrance to the Hawkesbury River to the north, and the Royal National Park to the south. The distance between Palm Beach on Pittwater and Cronulla just above the national park is 72 km. That's about as far as the distance from Cheshunt, north of London, to Crawley, well to the south of the capital. More striking still is the distance that Sydney extends to the west. From the CBD to the western extremity of the Metropolitan area, just past Penrith, is 55 km. Heading west from London, that would take you from Trafalgar Square, past Maidenhead and well on your way to

Reading. The Australian Statistical Geography Standard defines the Greater Sydney area as 12,369 km2 (4,776 square miles), of which only 67 km2 (26 square miles) is the City of Sydney, that bit that the world thinks of as Sydney. Half of one percent of the area takes up 99% of the world's attention. The area of Greater London is 1,572 km2 (607 square miles). Greater Sydney is nearly eight times the size of Greater London, but with about 60% of the population.

Sydney is a highly multi-cultural place, some even describe it as an Asian city. Cultural enclaves proliferate. 38% of the residents of Cabramatta were born in Vietnam. Leichhardt is well-known for its Italian influence, and Bankstown is famous for its Lebanese community. If you go to Warringah Mall on the Northern Beaches, you will hear English accents everywhere. It's a British enclave, although most don't recognise it as such. Poms don't really see themselves as foreigners in Australia.

Monday, 10th March 2025. Hyde Park Plaza, Sydney, NSW.

Premier League: Tottenham Hotspur 2 AFC Bournemouth 2

Captaining the team for this fixture was Christian Romero, finally back from injury. A lift for the home crowd and the rest of the team, surely? Sadly not. I could have played better than Romero did for the first five minutes, during which he presented the Bournemouth attackers with two excellent opportunities, which Vicario did well to save. As Ange said afterwards, Romero "grew into the game".

Despite being carved open on multiple occasions in the first half, it was not until the 42nd minute that Bournemouth took a deserved lead and went into the break one up. On the hour, Romero being withdrawn and replaced by VDV, received the loudest cheer of the day, presumably for introducing VDV and not the relief of seeing Romero being put out of his misery. Despite this upgrade, Bournemouth were soon two up.

It was at this point that lady luck favoured Spurs. A wildly inaccurate cross from Sarr sailed over the goalkeeper and into the far corner for 1-2. The Bournemouth goalkeeper couldn't do much about that one, but with 84 minutes on the clock, he made a critical intervention. With Sonny bearing down on the ball in the penalty area but heading away from goal, the keeper made the cardinal sin of getting anywhere near the attacker. Sonny did an excellent job of receiving the contact in such a way that the referee had no alternative but to point to the spot. Picking himself up to take the kick, Sonny dispatched a laughably poor spot kick which bounced before it went in. Fortunately, the Bournemouth keeper compounded his error by diving out of the way enthusiastically as Sonny's effort just about crept over the line. We escaped with a 2-2 draw.

I have a confession to make. Hyde Park Plaza, where we were staying in Sydney, is a ten-minute walk from the Surry Hills Hotel. Earlier in the season a 1am kick-off would have seen me down there, searching out other Spurs supporters to share the experience with. But I'm losing faith. I went to bed and watched the game in the morning. And I was pleased I did, because the team gave another miserable performance.

It pains me to say it but I am right on the verge of going full #Angeout. The team has no shape, no obvious tactics and very little spirit. I started the season with a tank full of credit for Ange as a man and what he has achieved in his career. But the low fuel light is flashing, and it feels like I'm going to stop before reaching the end of the road. We have a few nights left in Sydney before we head down to Melbourne for the Grand Prix weekend. But before that, it's the second leg against AZ. Our season is teetering on the brink.

> **Friday, 14th March 2025. Mornington Peninsula, Victoria.**
>
> **Europa League: Tottenham Hotspur 3 AZ 1**
>
> With Kulusevski being the only first choice player out injured, we had a near full strength team on the field, with both Romero and VDV finally reunited to fill the centre back roles. And it showed. Spurs looked far more assured than in recent games. The high press forced an error and a nice lay off from Solanke saw Odobert fire into the roof of the net, his first goal for the club.
>
> A neat finish from Maddison shortly after the break put us ahead on aggregate and looking comfortably in control. But this wouldn't have been Spurs without a bit of drama. With AZ unable to create any chances themselves, Bissouma and Bergvall contrived to put one on a plate for them and it was all level again. This was Spurs' night, though. A deserved winner came courtesy of Odobert's second of the game and we were through. This was a good night, keeping our season alive at least for another month as we head towards the quarterfinals of the competition.

So it's a stay of execution for Ange and I'm willing to put #Angeout on ice for now. The only hope of success this season rests on the Europa League and we're hanging on in there.

Not Such a Grand Prix

The Victorian Government spends around $100 million per year to host the Formula 1 Grand Prix, a sum they claim creates a net positive economic return to the state. Over 465,000 fan visits were recorded this year, although with many attending on more than one day, the number of unique visitors would be less. That certainly creates a lot of economic activity. Whether it's enough to cover the size of the investment is a matter of conjecture. There's no doubt that a healthy share of the Victorian government's motivation is about reputation and brand more than economics, or at least casts a very wide net across how the economic value is assessed. You'd think that in spending all of that money, the powers that be would want to put on a very good event indeed. After all, Melbourne does the tennis brilliantly. The quality and location of the venues make the entire event an extension of the life of the city. Getting in and out is simple, and getting there is a short walk from the CBD, or a free tram ride if you prefer. Surely the Grand Prix would be at least as good. Sadly, it wasn't. We spent more time queuing than watching motor racing.

Our first day at the event was Saturday. With the mercury pushing the mid 30s, we were grateful for the respite from the blistering hot sun provided by intermittent cloud cover. After taking the train into Southern Cross Station, our first queue of the day was for the free tram service provided to shuttle us to the event. An entry level queue this one. It was more of an extended tram stop experience, enhanced by temporary barriers sending us halfway up Spencer Street and back. We had expected to encounter our second queue of the day at the turnstile of Gate 1 when we reached the entrance to Albert Park but, to our surprise, it was just a simple swipe of the Apple wallet and we were in.

Any disappointment that queue aficionados may have felt at the gate would have been assuaged by what was waiting for us at the cross track bridge. Having purchased grandstand seats in the Brabham Stand, we were required to cross the track. To prevent patrons from having to play chicken and run across the track between the cars, the organisers had provided a bridge. With the evident intention of creating a classic queuing experience, they seriously undersized the capacity of the structure. As we approached the bridge, we could see one of those sheep pen-like areas perfected at Disney World, where a queue folds back and forth before accessing the main event. At first we thought we could walk straight into the sheep pens but our path was interrupted by an enthusiastic volunteer guide pointing us toward the back of the queue, about 100m up the path.

Joining at the back, we shuffled our way back towards the sheep pens and our eventual destination, the undersized bridge. This queue turned out to be far more interesting and innovative than we ever could have imagined. Tantalisingly, the 100m path section took us right back to the sheep pens, but just as we thought we were going to enter them, a whole new section of queue revealed itself to us. Across the park we headed, elongating the queue and causing a most unseemly fast walk to break out. Taking our directions from some young people in high viz vests who barely seemed in control of the situation, we took a hairpin turn around a tree and a chicane around some bins before heading back towards the bridge. Finally, we entered the sheep pens for our last few turns before traversing the track as the Formula 3 cars roared beneath our feet.

On race day we did the whole thing again but with the added ingredients of wind, rain and cold. With the venue being completely unprepared for rain, and no sign of cover to shelter under, we spent the whole day wet and cold. As the commentator said in my earpiece whilst we watched the race, "they say you get four seasons in one day in Melbourne. Today they've all been horrible." We braved the conditions to watch what turned out to be quite an entertaining race. The upside of what was otherwise a pretty miserable experience was that the rain caused a lot of the cars to crash which, let's be honest, is what all motor racing fans love to see. Oh, and Lando beat Max, which was also good. As the race ended, the sun briefly burst through the clouds to a cheer from the crowd. Whereupon it quickly went in again to be replaced with a dark cloud and a final dump of rain to ensure we went home thoroughly drenched.

After a warm shower, I declined the opportunity to stay up past midnight for kickoff and watched the Fulham game when I woke up in the morning.

Monday, 17th March 2025. Mornington Peninsula, Victoria.

Premier League: Fulham 2 Tottenham Hotspur 0

VDV's time is clearly being carefully managed as he spent this game on the bench, Davies coming in to partner Romero at the heart of the defence. Ange gave Gray his first opportunity to play in the holding midfield position.

The first half was a scrappy affair, with errors happening all over the pitch from both teams. A real mid-table scrap. With Bergvall and Sonny introduced at half-time, Spurs looked a lot more lively, creating a host of chances, although none that looked like actually producing the desired result.

As the game looked like it was drifting towards Spurs' first goalless draw for years, Fulham scored with a neat strike after some lax defending. Any hope of a comeback was snuffed out late on when Ryan Sessegnon turned Davies inside out and, showing a level of competence he rarely displayed when he played for us, poked the ball past Vicario and into the top corner.

The contrast between this match and the AZ victory was quite stark. With VDV on the pitch and our first choice team playing with commitment, we look like a half-decent team. Otherwise we look bang average.

CHAPTER 9

April 2025: Dignity or Silverware

Suffering For My Art

I started writing this book with what has now been revealed to be an insane level of optimism. Committing my emotional welfare to Tottenham Hotspur and Ange seemed like a surefire way to find another level of joy in my life. Somewhere along the line, it's all gone horribly wrong. Is this because of the underlying cultural malaise that has made the club unmanageable? Or has Ange succumbed to the Peter Principle, the idea that in their career everyone gets promoted to their first level of incompetence?

Before the Europa League victory that sent our season staggering on, at least for another month, I seriously considered giving up on this whole writing venture. I no longer thought anyone would be interested in reliving this miserable season, a view that was reinforced when I pitched the book to a couple of specialist sports publishers. David, at Legends Publishing in the UK, certainly confirmed my fears.

"Thanks for sending the details through and the sample chapters, however, I don't think this is one for us with the chance of sacking at any time and 2024/25 being a season to forget rather than one fans will want to relive in text." was his expert opinion. A second reply came from a sports publisher based in Melbourne, Slattery Media Group. Geoff Slattery himself replied, which suggests the Group might actually just be old Geoff sat in his kitchen. Nevertheless, Geoff was a bit more encouraging, and I was grateful for his positive reply.

"I enjoyed your writing style and long-time commitment to the club, however, this sort of book is not in my expertise." This giant of the publishing world enjoyed my writing style. Maybe I'm onto something after all.

Having written close to 50,000 words already, I've decided not to give up. I've reframed this book to be a survival story, in classic memoir style. The narrative arc of the story will reach its conclusion in the next couple of months, in Frankfurt, or possibly even Bilbao. And I am going to be here to tell the story, regardless of whether anyone will be reading.

Over the last six weeks, I have been doing an online course with the Australian Writers Centre on memoir writing and personal storytelling. Something I might have thought to do before starting the book! The tutor gives us feedback on a writing assignment that we have to submit every week, and in doing so she emphasises that as writers we are all artists. Her feedback is just her opinion and we are quite at liberty to ignore it if it is contrary to our artistic intent. Which is all very well, but now I'm suffering for my art and for my football team. And I'm supposed to be enjoying a relaxing and happy new stage of life.

It was a relief that this week there is an international break. It'll be Thomas Tuchel's first game in charge of England and he's threatening to get the players to perform as if they're playing in the Premier League. Not like they're playing some kind of chess with a ball, which brought Gareth Southgate so close to actually winning something. Not to worry that he didn't, they knighted him anyway.

After all the fixture congestion earlier in the season, there's now been a 17 day gap between the Fulham defeat and the next match, no doubt another defeat, at Chelsea.

Friday, 4th April 2025. Coogee Beach, Sydney.

Premier League: Chelsea 1 Tottenham Hotspur 0

Ange re-united VDV and Romero for our visit to Chelsea, a ground where we never win and, on this occasion, never looked like breaking the curse. Second best for most of the first half, it was a relief to get to half-time with no goals on the scoreboard. Only 5 minutes into the second half, to no one's surprise, Chelsea scored. More surprising was an apparent goal from Sarr, a strike from distance that the Chelsea keeper should have stopped. Ange then created the biggest talking point of the match when he cupped his ear to the Spurs fans who had given him stick for bringing on Sarr, in place of the ever impressive Bergvall. It was all a bit embarrassing when replays showed Sarr had assaulted the defender to win the ball and VAR chalked off the goal. Ange's claim that he had merely been encouraging the Spurs fans fooled nobody. The game petered out to another miserable but unsurprising defeat.

Surely the visit of Southampton, possibly the worst side ever to grace the Premier League, will provide some respite.

Hope Springs

The international break provided welcome relief from the anguish of following Spurs and I had cause for celebration. Both of my 'children' held engagement parties, George having also announced his engagement and providing the prospects of two weddings in 2026. Anna's party was the previous weekend, during the international break, and George's this weekend. It's funny how people refer to their sons and daughters as their children, even when they have become adults. If I'd said both my adults held engagement parties you wouldn't have known what I was talking about.

Anna and Ben's party was at a cool bar in Martin Place, George and Erin's in Erin's aunt's beautiful apartment overlooking the coastline just north of Coogee. It was for this reason that I watched both the Chelsea and Southampton games in a Coogee Beach hotel.

Sunday, 6th April 2025. Coogee Beach, NSW.

Premier League: Tottenham Hotspur 3 Southampton 1

Ange rested VDV, making room for the ever-dependable Davies, in what was a strong line-up. Ange's preferred midfield selection has finally settled down, featuring Bergvall, Bentancur and Maddison. It's an incredible feat for the young Bergvall to have gained this first choice position at his age and in his first season with the club. Against a predictably weak Southampton team, Spurs played dominant front foot football in the first half and their efforts were rewarded with a brace from Brennan Johnson, finding his scoring boots again after injury.

The second half was a different matter. Now playing within themselves, Spurs let Southampton back into the game and conceded a goal. For most of the half, you couldn't tell which team was the worst the Premier League has ever seen and which was just the worst Spurs team the premier league has ever seen. There really wasn't that much in it. A late penalty, competently dispatched by Tel, gave the score a respectable appearance, but in truth it had been another poor display.

I've been trying my hand at different genres of writing and this week, to cheer myself up, I thought I'd give comedy a go. With Spurs' season going so badly off course, the situation at the club felt like great subject matter for satire:

One Flew Over The Tottenham Hotspur Stadium

The Tottenham Hotspur board meeting was coming towards the last couple of items on the agenda, and Daniel Levy was feeling very pleased with himself.

"I think we can all agree it has been another successful season," he said to anyone still listening. "We still have the highest ticket prices, I remain the highest paid CEO and we have lots of concerts lined up to support our financial diversity strategy. Our reliance on that dreadful football team is reducing every season."

The Board, as usual, hung on his every word. "Yes, your honour, I mean Daniel," one of them said.

"Now, the last item on the agenda is the stadium naming rights. Who is going to report?"

An unremarkable little man, with no actual personality but a propensity to agree with everything Levy said, raised his hand.

"We have three bids," he said.

There had been three bidders preparing feverishly to take advantage of this unbelievable opportunity. So unbelievable in fact, that nobody had shown any genuine interest since the stadium opened six years before. Levy had had to float some big names to the media to get anyone interested. Amazon, Meta... all utterly ridiculous.

The first bidder was Qatar Airways. At their recent board meeting, they received a report on the matter from a senior partner at PWC, a company once of high repute.

"Etihad and Emirates have already nabbed two of the top stadiums. Our recommendation is not to miss the boat this time," he said as he reached his twentieth PowerPoint slide.

"Get on with it," said the chair of the Qatari business, "the bar's open."

"We have been to look at Tottenham Hotspur and it is the finest football club in the land," he continued.

"You didn't go and see them play then?" interjected the Qatari, now wishing he had paid extortionately over the odds for McKinsey, like he normally did.

"No, that is true, but the stadium is magnificent and they have the best training facilities in the land," the PWC Partner stated. As usual, he had missed the point. "How much money do you have to bid?" he asked.

"We've as much money as we want, you imbecile. We're owned by a sovereign wealth fund."

"I'm afraid that isn't how it works," the PWC partner replied, mopping the sweat from his brow.

"Well, it worked for Manchester City so it can work for Tottenham," the Qatari said, signing off on a multi-million dollar bid.

The second group preparing a proposal, surprisingly to some, was INEOS.

Sir Jim Ratcliffe was talking to his board. "Nobody has noticed that I'm really a Southampton fan," he gloated. "It's tough supporting such a terrible team, although we at least matched Tottenham in the second half the other day."

The INEOS plan to subvert the Premier League had worked wonders at Manchester United. "Bringing in that idiot Amorim and sacking all the tea ladies has been such fun," declared Ratcliffe. "Let's have a go at Tottenham next."

"That's a great idea. We've already sold the suckers a deal to promote that ridiculous 4x4 vehicle you came up with, Jim," said one of his lackeys. "They even put our name on the seats that the coaches sit on."

"I know right," said Sir Jim, "so many coaches and so little coaching!"

The lackey had another thought. "We'll tell them that INEOS stands for 'I know everything about Spurs'"

"You idiot," said Sir Jim, "that would be INEAS".

After further debate in which the INEOS board hung on his every word, Sir Jim signed-off on a bid.

The third and most surprising bid was prepared by the #LevyOut movement. At a clandestine meeting in the leader's flat, on the second floor above a kebab shop on the Tottenham High Road, they hatched a plan.

"The club has been very good at extending the fan base around the world," the leader said.

"Incredible really, given how bad the team is," a follower chipped in.

"The plan is to use the strength of the fan base to raise funds. We are going to crowdsource a bid for the stadium naming rights. If every Spurs fan who is discontent with how the team is going puts in a fiver, we should be in with a shot."

The committee agreed it was a brilliant idea. They spent the rest of the evening discussing what name they would give to the stadium.

Back at the Tottenham Hotspur board meeting, the unremarkable individual with no personality concluded his presentation of the bids.

"So, let me get this right," said Levy. "The Qataris are offering to give us access to their sovereign wealth fund, but there's a risk that we might contravene 115 regulations and get thrown out of the league?"

"Correct your honour, I mean Mr Levy."

"Too big a risk, I'd say. It's down to the other two. Now our good friend Sir Jim is offering five million a year to call it the INEOS stadium with the tagline 'I know everything about Spurs', I rather like that."

"But surely it should be INEAS," said the unremarkable man, for once daring to contradict his glorious leader.

"Good point," said Levy, "and that sounds a bit too much like 'in the arse', I'm not falling for that trick," he said, suddenly suspicious of Sir Jim's motives.

"Remind me again who the third bid came in from," said Levy.

"It's a mysterious group who simply style themselves #LO," the assistant said, "they have offered six million a year for three years."

Levy's eyes lit up, an extra million of income! "What do they want to call the stadium?" he asked.

"Now let me remind myself," said the unremarkable assistant, digging through his paperwork. "I know the acronym was WHLS."

"Well, that's not very original," said Levy. "The White Hart Lane Stadium. Why would they pay so much money to call it that?"

"Er, no. Here we are," said the assistant, "they want to call it the 'We Hate Levy Stadium' sir," the man said, a bit embarrassed.

"The what?" said Levy.

"The 'We Hate Levy Stadium' sir, or WHLS."

"How much more than Sir Jim have they offered?" asked Levy.

"A million a year for three years, sir."

"Sounds good to me," said Levy, signing off the deal.

"Now, AOB?" Levy asked, keen to finish the meeting and go to review his bank balance.

"Just one thing," said a new Non-Executive Director. "Shouldn't we have a report about the football team?" He had not been there long enough to understand the club's priorities.

"We normally leave that to the 'non revenue earning sub-committee', but seeing as you ask, do we have a report from the Greek?"

"The Greek, sir?"

"Yes, that postecogoo guy we took on."

"He's Australian, sir,"

"With a name like postalogaloo? He's not called Bruce is he?"

"No sir,"

"Anyway, what does it matter? Wherever he's from, he hasn't got a clue what he's doing. Where did we get him from?"

"Celtic, sir."

"What idiot signed that off?"

"You did, sir."

"Right, well, what does his report say?"

"It says we won at the weekend against a very strong opponent."

"Fuck me. How did that happen?" Levy asked. "Who was this strong team that we managed to overcome?"

"Southampton, sir. The report says that we played them off the park for the first half but due to their greater strength in depth, they matched us in the second."

"Well, that's all very encouraging," Levy said. "Ok, meeting over."

Levy smiled and opened his HSBC app as he left the room. It had been another outstanding day at the office.

Hope springs eternal and next up felt like the most important game of the season so far; the first leg of the Europa League quarter-final.

Friday, 11th April 2025. Gilgandra, NSW.

Europa League: Tottenham Hotspur 1 Eintracht Frankfurt 1

Except for Kulusevski, Ange had his full squad available and put out what he believes to be his strongest team. Vicario, Porro, VDV, Romero, Udogie, Maddison, Bergvall, Bentancur, Johnson, Solanke and Sonny. On paper, it was a strong line-up and for once they performed somewhere close to their potential.

Frankfurt started strongly and scored in the seventh minute. Our defence was slow to close down Ekitike, a dangerous striker, who scored with a crisp shot from the edge of the box. In an even first half, both sides made chances, and it was a subtle back foot flick through his legs from Porro that brought the equaliser.

In the second half, Spurs played the best football they have produced for months, creating several chances and striking the woodwork twice. A fabulous shot from distance by Bergvall hit the corner of the upright and crossbar, and a Bentancur header from a corner struck the bar. The final whistle brought mixed feelings. A strong display, but not the result we wanted.

The Frankfurt game proved there's a half decent side in there, despite what we have seen in the Premier League. Hope is still there, desperately being clung on to by millions of fans around the world.

Hanging by a Thread

We finally got around to replacing our stolen bikes. At first, we hoped that the Queensland Police would miraculously track down the thief and return our original bikes to their rightful owners. Then we had to overcome the emotional shock of being victims before we could get excited about spending a significant amount of money just to get back something that we should still have had. Having reached that point, we got back into research mode to decide which bikes we would buy.

We bought our previous bikes on a whim at The Hairy Marron in Margaret River. We just chose a couple of bikes they had in store and seemed to fit the bill. This time, being far more experienced e-bike users made the selection process more complicated. First, we tried a couple of shops in Dubbo. Then, whilst in Sydney, we checked out the city stores, both on Clarence Street. There is one for each of the major suppliers; Giant and Trek. And we took the Metro out to Waterloo where there is a large independent store. We discovered that the problem with buying bikes in a city store is that there's generally one person who knows what they're talking about, and a bunch of others who pretend to but ultimately hand you off to the person who does. If you can wait that long. In Waterloo we couldn't, and walked out after about 20 minutes. In the Clarence Street stores, one was just arrogant and the other quite pleasant, but only really wanted to give us one option.

Driving back from Sydney, Tracy was keen to get into the Giant store in Mudgee. We had used them before to get my previous bike fixed when I had tricked it into going faster than the 25 km/hr restriction imposed in Australia. You can make them go faster but, as I discovered, after a while the computer shuts down and you have to send it away to be reset. Tracy had spotted a great discounted price on the bike she fancied on the Giant Mudgee website. The price seemed to even surprise them, but they honoured it, and also helped me select a bike that would meet my needs. We ordered them there and then; two full dual suspension mountain e-bikes. We were happy to have bought them in Mudgee. There's something quite rewarding about supporting a small business where you are dealing directly with the owners, and we know we will get good after-sales service. It's something we've become more aware of since acquiring our own family business.

Picking the bikes up ten days later, we also purchased two of the highest standard D locks available, three chain locks and an alarm/tracker fitted to each bike. We also bought insurance. Now it's us against the thieves and they are going to have to work a lot harder to relieve us of our wheels this time than they did on the Gold Coast.

Sunday, 13th April 2025. Gilgandra Caravan Park, NSW.

Premier League: Wolverhampton Wanderers 4 Tottenham Hotspur 2

Ange put out a bit of a makeshift team to protect the likes of VDV, Bergvall and Bentancur and was immediately punished with a goal from Wolves in two minutes. A lacklustre first half performance ended 2-0 to Wolves when Spence, actually our best player, put into his own net. Vicario was having a less than stellar evening, contributing to both Wolves' goals.

In the second half, there were more downs than ups for Spurs despite both teams scoring twice. A few late substitutions saw game time for Bergvall and Bentancur, and welcome returns from injury for Richarlison (quite welcome) and Kulusevski (very welcome).

It was another abject performance. All media reports now focused on how long Ange would survive, the consensus being that he was hanging by a thread called the Europa League. Would the second leg in Frankfurt be his last game, many wondered?

Friday, 18th April 2025. Wagga Wagga, NSW.

Europa League: Eintracht Frankfurt 0 Tottenham Hotspur 1

Unsurprisingly, Ange put out his strongest team, the same as for the first leg. Kulusevski was not quite fit enough to start, but otherwise most Spurs fans would have concurred with Ange's selection. It soon became apparent that this was going to be a very different Spurs display. Safety first, get it up the field, keep the full backs tucked in, play with the ball when we have it, but get behind it when we don't. Pragmatism had finally broken out in the ranks, and it was working.

A fairly balanced first half was coming to an end when the seminal moment of the match occurred. A long ball into the box from Romero was headed goalward by Maddison a split second before the goalkeeper arrived on the scene and wiped him out. It was a nailed on penalty. Except to the referee, that is. It is at times like this that VAR shows its value – a clear and obvious mistake was overturned and a penalty awarded. Dominic Solanke stepped up, watched the goalkeeper dive out of the way, and knocked the ball into the space he had just vacated. Maddison went off with a combination of a sore leg and concussion to be replaced by a rusty but hard-working Kulusevski.

The second half was an excellent defensive display. Other than three chances, all of which were fluffed by the opposition right back Kristensen, the defence stood firm. The final whistle saw wild celebrations from the team and the away supporters. Even Ange joined in, no doubt happy to still have a job and the opportunity to fulfil his second season trophy prediction.

The question on the minds of most supporters following this win was why don't we play like that more often? Finally Ange had forsaken his style of play for something that was self-evidently more likely to succeed, and it had. Was it his secret path to salvation? Nobody will care where we end up in the league if we win a trophy, and with it a golden ticket into next season's Champions League. Will we see this style of play against Bodø/Glimt, our unlikely semi-final opponents? It will only be a couple of weeks before we find out.

Another Routine Defeat

Most welcome news has reached us from Alfie. The CPS approved the laying of charges against DW and they have summoned him to appear in court on 30th June. The charges are fraud and theft. Given the position of authority he was entrusted with, and the vulnerable nature of his victim, we expect the case will be at the more serious end of the scale for each of the charges. The initial hearing is to be in a magistrate's court where he will be required to plead. If he pleads guilty, it will go straight to sentencing, although this may be done in the crown court, given the serious nature of the crimes. If he pleads not guilty, we expect the case will go to the crown court for trial.

We've been trying to second guess what he's going to do. If he has any sense, he'll plead guilty and try to argue for a non-custodial sentence. But we know he doesn't have much sense, so we expect he will plead not guilty, which at least from his perspective will kick the can down the street for another year or two before it comes to trial. I can imagine him changing his plea at the last minute at that point. But this is all speculation. Whatever he does, we are putting our faith in the British justice system to find him guilty and pass a suitable sentence. Anything less than prison will be a great disappointment to us.

I didn't intend to leave a cliffhanger, but this is where this story thread is going to end, at least as far as this book is concerned. Maybe I'll have to write the story of next season so that I can tell everyone how the story finishes. Otherwise, I'll put it on my website.

For Easter we headed south from the caravan park in Winston and had a few nights off-grid at a very pleasant free campsite called Oura Beach, on the banks of the Murrumbidgee River. By off-grid I mean we were using all the motorhome's capacity to provide for us, with no connection to water or power. We managed five days, our longest period in this mode since we acquired him. I did nip out once to fill his water tanks, and nursed the generator into life to keep the batteries charged.

Moving on again on Easter Monday, we managed to find a really lovely little park in the King Valley wine region in northern Victoria. Which is where I watched the next game, home to Forest.

> **Tuesday, 22nd April 2025. Moyhu Caravan Park, Victoria.**
>
> **Premier League: Tottenham Hotspur 1 Nottingham Forest 2**
>
> Premier League defeats have become so commonplace now I can barely even be bothered to write about them. Once again we went behind early, this time when a poor corner clearance from Porro in the fifth minute led to a deflected shot which Vicario flapped all around, but failed to stop. Forest had already had another chalked off for offside when a routine cross into the box met Chris Woods' head just before Vicario arrived on the scene, leaving his goal wide open.
>
> Thereafter, Forest were quite happy to let us have the ball and defend manfully whilst we once again failed to make many meaningful chances. Tel and Spence combined well down the left, and Odobert plugged away down the right, but when the goal came, it was far too late. In the 87th minute, Richarlison had his customary single moment of competence per match and scored a very tidy header. Forest had no trouble seeing out the remaining minutes and it had been another routine defeat.

Once again, the press coverage this week spoke of Ange leaving at the end of the season. The discussion being whether he walks out, is sacked or leaves by 'mutual consent'. The big question is, will he leave as a total failure or as the first manager to deliver a trophy in 17 years? And if he were to achieve that unlikely result, will he become untouchable, too popular for Levy to sack?

I believe Ange is a good man, but the evidence leads me to question whether he is competent to manage at this level. For him, for me and for all the long-suffering Spurs supporters, I really am hoping there'll be a trophy for Ange to point to at the end of the season. A defeat in the final is the least we should expect now. If we can't overcome the team fifth in the Norwegian league over two legs, we deserve nothing from the season. And with only a week to wait, it won't be long to find out how we go in the first leg at home. All we have to negotiate before then is a visit to champions-elect Liverpool. Now that's going to be an interesting team selection.

Sad news

Our next destination was a return to Albury. Having never been there before the stag weekend, fate had conspired to prompt an early return. Our good friends Ally and Lou came over from the UK to attend the Grand Prix and could not return home when planned after Ally suffered a medical emergency. We took the opportunity to spend some time with them and booked an Airbnb in central Albury. The week was spent chilling out and teaching them canasta, a card game that Tracy and I have discovered can easily become addictive.

Standing at the breakfast bar late one morning, I took a call on my mobile.

"Is that Andy?"

"Yes."

"It's Jason Whyte, Cam's brother." Up to this point, I didn't know Cam had a brother. After my conversation with Steve Palmer a few weeks before, I feared the worst.

"Hi, how are you?"

"Yeah, ok thanks. Look, I just need to give you an update on Cam. His cancer's got to a point where they've given him just a couple of months. He asked me to call a few people to let them know."

I relayed the news to Tracy, and we shared a moment of contemplation. Even though we knew it was coming, we were desperately sad to hear the news. Cam was a good friend to both of us. He'd always been welcoming when we went to the Surry Hills Hotel to watch matches. He'd been to a party at our apartment, even though we know social settings like that didn't come easily to him. We resolved to visit him at the Chris O'Brien Lifehouse, where he was receiving palliative care, when we arrived back in Sydney.

News like this puts everything into perspective. I've always hated that quote about football being more important than life and death. It's puerile nonsense. And ironic that it was Bill Shankly who said it, given our next opponents...

Monday, 28th April 2025. Albury, NSW.

Premier League: Liverpool 5 Tottenham Hotspur 1

With the champions in waiting needing only a point to confirm the crown, Ange rested VDV, Romero and Porro, leaving the worthy but inadequate pairing of Davies and Danso to hold back the tide of the most prolific attack in the league. The only surprise was that we scored first. A strong header at the back post by Solanke put the ball back across the keeper and into the net to silence the Anfield crowd. For three whole minutes, the possibility of a shock delay to the home crowd's celebrations seemed a possibility before normal service was resumed and, 20 minutes later, Liverpool went into a 2–1 lead.

Thereafter, it became a question of how many Liverpool would rack up and how embarrassed Spurs would be. Inevitably, Mo Salah netted before Destiny Udogie made it onto the scoresheet, deflecting a rebound from Vicario into his own net.

It felt like the club had forsaken its dignity to protect the potential of silverware. Most fans won't care about that, if success arrives in the Europa League. It would be a welcome end to the trophy drought. But if Spurs fans are honest with themselves, they have to concede that the Europa League is simply a competition for the teams not good enough to get into the Champions League. Watching the likes of PSG, Barcelona and Inter reminds me of the gulf between us and the elite of Europe.

I need to rouse myself from this apathy! The first leg of the semi-final of a major tournament is nearly upon us and glory beckons...

Friday, 2nd May 2025. Albury, NSW.

Europa League: Tottenham Hotspur 3 Bodø/Glimt 1

A season-ending injury to Lucas Bergvall felt like a real blow to our chances of securing the Europa League trophy. It was a real sign of the progress he had made. His replacement by Bissouma, who most consider has had a patchy season at best, was a distinct downgrade. Losing Sonny to injury would normally similarly be seen as a big problem but his form this season has also been variable. Richarlison and Tel have become the left wing replacements, this evening both getting a half.

Spurs looked far superior to their Norwegian opponents, outmuscling them and controlling the game. A Brennan Johnson goal from the first attack settled the nerves and domination across the park led to a second from Maddison. Ange's tactics were more direct than normal, trusting our forwards to win duels from long balls up the park.

Despite the team mainly playing in containment mode in the second half, Romero got into the box and drew a foul, spurring VAR into action and presenting Solanke with the opportunity to put us three up from the spot. With ten minutes to go and 3-0 to the good, it looked like the tie was already in the bag when, in true Spurs fashion, we conceded from Bodø/Glimt's only shot on target. 3-1 then to take into the Arctic Circle.

Once again, Spurs played well when it mattered. It really is like watching two different clubs. I guess I should be grateful that at least one of them looks competitive.

CHAPTER 10

May 2025: The Final Whistle Blows

We DID it!

I've been thinking about the duality of our Premier League and Europa League campaigns. Something really strange is happening and I don't understand why. Ange has been telling everyone this week that you have to play differently in cup football, particularly in European competitions, but I'm not convinced. I admit I'm far from being an expert on the theories and tactics of the game, but I've watched a lot of football in my life and I think my confusion is warranted.

What I don't understand is why a style of play that works in Europe can't also work in the Premier League. And given that we've lost most of our games in the Premier League, wouldn't it at least be worth a try? The much vaunted Angeball has been ineffective, or more likely outdated, this season. Counter-attacking has become a winning formula in the Premier League, nuanced with strong defence and fluidity in midfield. Ange has been sticking to his principles and we've all been suffering the consequences. Happy to be more flexible and pragmatic in cup competitions, he's hit upon a style that suits the strengths of the players.

If the team were an individual, it would be deemed to have severe mental health issues. And the diagnosis would be Dissociative Identity Disorder (DID). In common parlance, a dual personality. It's a complex psychological condition where a person experiences two or more distinct personality states which can control their behavior at different times. Such a diagnosis would normally lead to intensive therapy with an intention of returning the individual to a more normal, balanced and singular personality. For Spurs, that won't happen until the season ends and Levy decides what happens next.

Sunday, 4th May 2025. Albury, NSW.

Premier League: West Ham United 1 Tottenham Hotspur 1

Ange put out a decidedly second string team for this 16th v 17th Premier League clash. With the clocks having changed in both Australia and the UK, a lunchtime kick-off in London translated to an 11pm start in Australia. I seriously considered going to bed and watching it in the morning, but a sense of loyalty kept me up.

The match started slowly, feeling more like a training game than a local derby. The general level of incompetence on display from both teams only matched the lack of endeavour. This was truly a dreadful game of football. Fittingly, the first goal came from an error by West Ham at the back. Tel pinched the ball from the defender and in a moment of quality unbefitting the occasion, crossed for a completely unmarked Odobert to score. Later in the half, West Ham contributed their one moment of competence when the always impressive Bowen swept into the box and put a close-range shot through Vicario's legs. For the rest of the game, mediocrity prevailed, and it was a blessed relief to all concerned when the referee blew the final whistle.

From Albury, we headed back in the general direction of Sydney and stopped to look at our nation's capital, Canberra. With the caravan parks close to the city not looking so inviting, we found a llama and alpaca sanctuary 20 minutes down the road and spent a couple of nights off-grid. Llamas, it turned out, are friendly animals, particularly if you have a carrot in your hand.

I've always thought of Canberra as a slightly dull city but it was nothing of the sort. Catching up with a friend for dinner, we ate at a Japanese-Peruvian restaurant. We weren't convinced this was actually a genuine style of cuisine but it turns out that it is, invented by Japanese immigrants to Peru in the late nineteenth and early twentieth centuries. It was wonderful. The restaurants in the city were thriving, the streets were humming with people going about their business. The quality of life in and around the city is higher than most Australians realise, with wonderful cultural and sporting facilities. We took advantage of the cycling infrastructure, including mountain bike trails in the hills outside the city and the cycle path that takes you around Lake Burley Griffin.

Despite Spurs' woeful performance in East London, it was always going to be the other personality that turned out for the biggest game of the season to date; the second leg of the Europa League semi-final. In the buildup to the match, there was much talk of Bodø/Glimt's impressive home record, the weather north of the Arctic Circle and the vagaries of playing on an artificial pitch. From the way supporters were fretting online you'd have thought the pitch was a giant banana skin, just waiting for a Spursy slip-up to disappoint us all. As a result, despite having a two goal lead from the first leg and a patently better team, nerves were on edge as the game kicked off.

Friday, 9th May 2025. Canberra, ACT.

Europa League: Bodø/Glimt 0 Tottenham Hotspur 2

An aggressive pressing game saw Spurs on the front foot from the off, the early territorial advantage settling nerves amongst supporters and evidently on the pitch too. The pattern of the game settled into Bodø/Glimt having most of the possession but failing to penetrate a comfortable Spurs defence. We were dominating the game without the ball, just the style of play that many Premier League teams played against us in the season, to great effect.

Nil-all at half-time, and it was feeling like all the concerns raised in the lead up to the game had been overstated. The match recommenced in a similar vein to the first half until, just after the hour, Romero leapt to head a corner goalward and Solanke pounced to toe poke past the goalkeeper. Get in! Spurs fans can even convince themselves that a three goal lead with less than half an hour to go does not represent a certain victory. But six minutes later, even the most sceptical fan could not ignore the inevitability of the outcome when Porro mis-hit a cross that struck the far post and went in. The game was effectively over at that point.

The mood amongst Spurs fans was transformed overnight. Footage of the players celebrating in front of a small but hardy bunch of away supporters, and in the changing rooms, were shared widely across social media. The club released a film of Ange talking to the players after the game. All of a sudden, doubts about his leadership have been put on ice and everyone associated with the club is behind him.

We are going to a major European final!

A Big Decision

A look back on my journey through the season reveals 28 different locations in which I watched a Spurs game. Now, with just two weeks and three matches to go, the end of the season beckoned. Ange has been trying to make the case that the poor form in the Premier League is linked to our success in the Europa League, and to an extent the Carabao Cup. I'm not sure I'm buying it. Regardless, the Premier League season is nearly over and it will be a blessed relief to see the back of it.

We needed to be in Sydney for Tracy to attend a board meeting in mid-May, so we picked somewhere halfway between Canberra and Sydney to break the journey. It was how I found myself parked up at an equestrian centre just outside Moss Vale, in the Southern Highlands, for the last Premier League game before the big final. I somehow knew it would not go well.

Sunday, 11th May 2025. Southern Highlands, NSW.

Premier League: Tottenham Hotspur 0 Crystal Palace 2

With Crystal Palace in the FA Cup final, both teams had a big match to look forward to. In Palace's case just seven days away, in our case ten. The difference in philosophy between the two managers was stark. Palace saw the benefit of keeping the first team together, an opportunity to inject a confidence boost before their big day. Ange rested all but three of the team that had won in Norway and fielded a decidedly second-rate team. The result was inevitable.

In a defensive display that plumbed new depths, Spurs played into the hands of Palace's attack, leaving the wings wide open and inviting attack after attack. With Gray looking lightweight and Bissouma in a lackadaisical mood, we also ceded the midfield. Going forward, we lacked any penetration and never looked like scoring. The only thing remarkable about Palace taking the lead just before half-time was that it had taken that

> long, two previous 'goals' having been disallowed. At the beginning of the second half, a lightning-quick break from Palace might not have resulted in a goal, had Bissouma decided to actually run back, but at 0–2, and with 42 minutes still to play, the outcome was inevitable. The return of Sonny after an hour at least saw the introduction of a player seen to be really trying to make something happen, which says more about the rest of them than it does about him.

We arrived back in Sydney and parked Winston at the Lane Cove Holiday and Caravan Park. Not having stayed there before, we were pleasantly surprised. Most caravan parks in cities are too tight on space and feel detached from nature. Despite being close to suburban business districts North Ryde and Macquarie Park, this one borders on the Lane Cove National Park, a green oasis that runs along the Lane Cove river, through the north western suburbs of Sydney.

Tracy was sick, having finally succumbed to a cough and cold that I had been fighting whilst we were in Albury. As a result, I went alone to see Cam at the Chris O'Brien Lifehouse.

Going to visit somebody with a terminal illness was not something I had previously experienced. I admit I was apprehensive as I drove over to the Lifehouse. What is the protocol? Do you talk about just normal things as if life would continue for both of us? Is it appropriate to raise the spectre of what death might mean, what might lie beyond? I decided to let Cam take the lead in where he wanted the conversation to go. Who was I to be concerned about my own feelings at such a time?

"Andy, hi!" Cam greeted me as I stuck my head around the door of room 9.16 on the top floor of the Lifehouse, a modern building in the Inner West completed in 2013. Cam always called me Andy, as many of my best friends do, even though I only ever introduce myself as Andrew. "Take a seat."

Cam already had a visitor, a friend from his time working on the railways, and they were in the middle of a conversation about cricket. It was a familiar topic and a comfortable start to the visit. I was immediately struck by Cam's appearance. He had lost 70kg and had a gaunt look that reflected his condition. As I looked into his eyes whilst we chatted, I could see that Cam was well and truly still with us, his spirit indomitable.

The friend left soon after I arrived, and Cam filled me in on a decision he had made.

"Have you heard the latest about my situation?" I wasn't sure if I had.

"I've decided to end things on my terms, it's all been signed-off." He was talking about voluntary assisted dying (VAD).

VAD became legal in New South Wales on 28th November 2023, the last state in Australia to implement it. The legislation allows people with a terminal illness to choose when to die, provided they are expected to live no more than six to twelve months.

"Was there much involved in getting it agreed?" I asked.

"No, I just met with my oncologist."

"What's the timeframe?"

"A couple of weeks."

I was struck by how calm and considered he was about the whole situation. It was clear that he had found peace with his decision.

The conversation moved on and we chatted about football. Characteristically, Cam asked about my son George, and Tracy's mum. He retained a concerned interest in others, despite his own plight.

"You've got the penthouse view from here," I said as I stood up to stretch my legs and observed the view of the city skyline through the window.

"I always believed in being kind and showing an interest in people," he told me. "I've been getting to know the nurses – they're all so wonderful – and they said they'd move me to a better room when one became available. That's how I was moved around to here." It was a simple example of Cam's philosophy. What goes around comes around. Be good to people and they'll pay you back with kindness.

I left that visit with a commitment to return the following week with Tracy. She has always had a great relationship with Cam, since he was so welcoming to her when she started joining me to watch games at the Surry Hills Hotel. He was like that with everyone, of course. It was just what he did.

My emotions were mixed as I walked down the corridor to the bank of glass lifts that whisk people up and down the Lifehouse's atrium. On the one hand, I was desperately sad. This was a really good man that was about to die too young. And yet, the way he was dealing with the situation was strangely uplifting. He had made me feel comfortable, despite the circumstances, and I had really enjoyed our chat. The resolve with which he had planned the end of his life was giving him some comfort. It was his way of dealing with the situation. But it also brought solace to me, and no doubt to the many other friends that visited him in his last weeks.

Bilbao

I returned to the Lifehouse with Tracy the following week. Cam remained in good spirits under the circumstances, although he looked physically more uncomfortable than when I saw him the previous week. He said he was not experiencing much pain but complained about a loss of bowel control.

We sat and chatted for two hours. At one point, Cam took a call from a priest who had been to see him previously and wanted to come in again later that day. That intervention prompted a more philosophical conversation. We talked about faith, and what exists beyond what we know.

"I'm a believer, but not practising," Cam told us.

We agreed there must be things that exist in some form that we don't know about. The notion that man knows everything about our world, and what lies beyond it, would be fanciful. Which leads to the conclusion that there must be things we don't understand. What influence those things have on us are unknown. Some choose to call that unknown God, and believe in a religion. That's their choice. The three of us, at that moment, were comfortable to accept that there are things we just don't know.

"I can't see that we are born, live our lives and then die without our soul continuing in some form. That just doesn't seem right," Cam said. The timeframe within which he might discover the answer to that question was getting shorter. He had set the date for his assisted dying for Monday 26th May 2025. Whether by chance or design, this would be the day on which the Spurs season would end (in Australian time, at least) and four days after the club's bid for European glory.

We embraced Cam and walked back along the corridor with tears in our eyes.

We had offered to help with preparations for the big night of the final at the Surry Hills Hotel but two of the Spurs faithful, Dave Towe and Nick Ieronimides, with Nick's son Christos, arranged to go into the Lifehouse to watch the game with Cam. Nick's streaming app provided access to a feed for the match and he'd worked out how to get it onto the big screen at the end of the bed, much to Cam's delight. Cam's only concern was that his friends would miss out on the atmosphere in the pub, another demonstration of his selfless approach to life.

The average attendance for a Sydney OzSpurs meet up to watch a game is around 30 to 40. I've been in for games at which only one or two others bothered to show up. Woolwich games get more like a couple of hundred, but it is when Spurs reach a cup final that we really find out how many fans are in the city. All of a sudden, they are everywhere.

The right thing to do was to hold the event at the Surry Hills Hotel. Nights like this are how we can reward the loyalty that the pub shows OzSpurs on other occasions, by opening their doors at all times of day and night for the hardy few. Nathan, the Sydney Chapter organiser, did a great job of putting arrangements in place to hold a ticketed OzSpurs members only event at the pub, the proceeds from the $5 a head ticket price going to the Lifehouse. The number of paid-up OzSpurs members increased as the demand for tickets grew, and the pub decided to increase capacity by opening the upstairs bar. OzSpurs sold 350 tickets in advance online and, at the pub's discretion, over 100 more were available to be sold on the night.

Tracy and I arrived at the Surry Hills Hotel at midnight, five hours ahead of the 5am kick-off. About 20 Spurs shirts could be seen dotted around the pub amongst a few of the pub's regulars. As we helped, checking new arrivals off the list and handing out wristbands, the numbers slowly increased. At 3am there was a big influx and the atmosphere began to build. At 4am a crew from Optus Sport arrived and I was assigned to liaise with them. With the game itself being streamed on Stan, a rival service, Optus Sport decided to do a 'watch along' from the Surry Hills Hotel, live streamed on YouTube. This involved three of their presenters chatting about the game whilst following it on an iPad, with the melee in the main bar behind them. Quite who was going to be watching three people talking about a game at 5am when the match itself could be watched on another service, I don't know, but they later told me they were happy with the viewing figures. Myself and Matt Zammitt were invited to briefly reprise our Fanzone punditry, together with Danny Joseph from Hobart who had joined us for the night, and the OzSpurs National weekend that was to follow.

Thursday, 21st May 2025. Surry Hills Hotel, Sydney.

Europa League Final: Tottenham Hotspur 1 Manchester United 0

The team was much as expected, with the one point of interest being Richarlison named ahead of Sonny on the left wing. This was undoubtedly a sign that despite having started against Aston Villa, Sonny was not fully fit. As the game started, it became clear that the match was not going to be a celebration of the beautiful game. In fact, it was a really ugly game. As befitted two teams that had collectively lost over 40 games in the Premier League, the winner was going to be the team that was the least incompetent on the night. The spectacle of the ball being given away repeatedly was regularly interrupted by the referee blowing his whistle, on some occasions justifiably.

The goal, when it came, was an appropriate reflection of the match. A ball into the box from Porro was directed towards Brennan Johnson, who threw a leg at it and missed. Not to be outdone, Luke Shaw, in attempting to play the ball without directing it into his own net, did just that, with his arm. Johnson waved his big toe towards the ball whilst Onana in the United goal flapped at it lamely. Somehow it crept inside the post, prompting Johnson to wheel away as if he'd scored the most important goal of his career. Whether he'd actually touched it on the way in was not clear, but nobody cared.

To say the pub 'went off' at this point is something of an understatement. In scenes not seen in the Surry Hills Hotel since the Lucas Moura winner in 2019, complete pandemonium broke out. With half-time only a few minutes away, the crowd remained in positive spirits through the break.

In the second half, Spurs simply gave up any real pretence of attack and it became clear that they were backing themselves to keep United at bay. The moment of the match arrived in the 66th minute when Vicario made a complete hash of catching a cross and contrived to accidentally head it to Hojland, who in turn headed it back towards an open goal. In a moment that will go down in Spurs history, to be talked about for decades to come, VDV anticipated what was going to happen and launched himself towards the goal. With the ball just about to cross the line at chest height, VDV, by this point in mid-air, extended his leg to intercept the ball with his shin and sent it back whence it had come. It felt like the moment when we realised United just weren't going to score.

With 15 minutes to go, Ange made it clearer than ever that the only way was defence when he took off Johnson, who had done his normal trick of contributing very little other than scoring a goal. On came Danso to make a five-man defence.

The game ended with a fine save by Vicario, leading to a corner for United. As the television commentator said, it was by now the eighth added minute of seven. In the Surry Hills Hotel some covered their eyes, others hugged loved ones. Nails were bitten, breath held. A last United attempt on goal with an overhead kick went beyond the far post and we all knew what was coming. Between leaving Vicario's boot and landing on a player's head, the referee would blow his whistle and 17 years of pain would be over.

Spurs had finally done it! Ange had fulfilled his second season prediction and Spurs supporters around the globe went into delirium. The consensus view on Ange's tenure swung instantly, suddenly he was a hero, and rightly so. His single-mindedness and dogged pursuit of a strategy had worked. The first trophy in 17 years, earning qualification for the Champions League next season to boot.

Social media went into overdrive, fans and media alike keen to share the story, pictures and video coming out of Bilbao. Much of it centred on Sonny winning his first trophy. Was there ever a player more deserving of success? A world-class player and a world-class human being.

And what about my emotional state? What I felt could best be described as contentment. It was our time again, at long last. I was happy for all the supporters who had waited so long to experience a moment like this. And happy that I'd won $220 with the bet I put on Spurs to win the Europa League at the beginning of the season.

Mostly, I was happy for one man. In his hospital bed on the 9th floor of the Lifehouse, Cam savoured the moment, with his friends in the room and with Tracy by text:

Tracy: For you (accompanied by a video of the fans celebrating at the pub and a heart emoji)

Cam: Unbelievable Tracy, outstanding performance I am speechless

Tracy: What a win

Cam: That it was, absolutely beautiful performance

The trophy win and the impending loss of our friend were a curious confluence of events. How could a game of football be of any significance in the context of the loss of a life? And yet the victory had brought joy to so many, including Cam himself. Ange had delivered glory, just when we needed it most.

The Last Goodbye

Until this point, I was still in two minds about whether to finish this book. I had been working on another book *Travels with Tracy* about the midlife gap year travels Tracy and I had been on for two years, and was preparing it for publication. My appetite for sharing the story of Spurs' season had waned beyond the point at which I had the enthusiasm to complete it.

But in the aftermath of the Europa League victory, and its coincidence with Cam's last days, I found new meaning and purpose in the endeavour. I resolved to complete the book, publish it as a tribute to Cam and donate all proceeds to the Chris O'Brien Lifehouse.

The day after the final saw the start of the OzSpurs National event in Sydney. It was set to be a weekend of celebrations. The first night 'meet and greet' was held upstairs in the Surry Hills Hotel. As the final was played on repeat on the television screens, old friends from around the country caught up, talked about the final and watched an online chat with the former player, Sandro. I mentioned to a few people my idea for the book and everyone was enthusiastic about it. Something was bothering me though, I wasn't feeling comfortable telling Cam's story without getting his explicit consent.

So, on Saturday morning I got out of bed, showered, and walked the 3 km to the Lifehouse from the Airbnb at Hyde Park we had rented for the National weekend. I was keen to have a few quiet minutes to talk about the book with Cam before any other visitors arrived.

It was a beautiful Sydney morning, and the route chosen by Apple Maps took me through the hallowed grounds of the University of Sydney, the sandstone buildings glowing in the autumn sunlight. When I arrived, Cam was still asleep. I went to get a coffee whilst he woke and was attended to by the nurses.

Unlike the bustling hive of activity I'd encountered during the week, on a Saturday morning the Lifehouse was eerily quiet. Fortunately, I discovered one leaf of the giant folding glass partition that separates the cafe from the lobby was open, and a skeleton staff was on hand to serve the occasional visitor and staff member in need of caffeine. As I sat with my coffee, I watched as visitors passed through the lobby, and I wondered about the story each would have to tell. Lifehouse is a world class cancer hospital, providing the full range of cancer services, from screening and prevention to the treatment of the most complex and rare cancers. Not all the people I saw would be there for someone in palliative care. At least I hoped they weren't.

Finally, I was allowed in to see Cam. From his position and demeanour, it was clear he was less comfortable again than when I had last seen him, just a few days before. I waited whilst he replied to a few messages that had come in on his phone overnight before we talked briefly about the Europa League final. Then I raised the subject of the book.

"The story is my emotional journey through the season. I'm keen to finish it now that we've ended the season on a high, but my emotions are tied up with your situation. So I wanted to ask if you're ok with me telling your story in the book? My plan is to donate the proceeds to the hospital."

"That's fine Andy," he seemed pleased with the idea, but was struggling with his discomfort.

"Will you make sure my brother and mum get a copy?" he asked. I told him I would.

"Do you have any reflections to share?" I asked. He gazed out of the window.

"No, not really. I've had a simple life, you might say, but a good one. I've met lots of great people like you and Tracy, and so many of the OzSpurs guys."

We talked about human connection and the legacy we leave through the influence we have on the people we meet along the way. And we talked about how supporting a football team brings people together. I could tell that the role he held in OzSpurs and the friendships he had made through the club were an important part of his life.

"Do you mind if I ask about how you reached the decision to choose when to go?" I asked.

He explained he didn't know about VAD until he was in a bad way and being cared for in the intensive care unit a few weeks before. It was about the time Steve had called me.

"If I could end it now with a pill, I would," he said to his oncologist. She then explained to him that there was a process he could follow if he wanted to choose when to go.

"It wasn't an easy decision," he said. He shifted his body in his discomfort. "I'm feeling pretty bad today. It's started." He was talking about the natural process. It was two days before the scheduled end.

That evening, the OzSpurs National continued with a four-hour harbour cruise. With the annual Vivid festival lighting up the city, about 60 Spurs fans set about celebrating the trophy win. Before the final, OzSpurs President Sean Bielski had commissioned a large Europa League Winners banner that was displayed proudly at the front of the dance floor.

"I told the guy that made it he should just bin it if we lost," he told me with a smile.

Somebody had done a good job of creating a Spurs playlist. Not only actual Spurs songs, but all those tunes that have been appropriated by the fans. Gimme Gimme Gimme "a ginger from Sweden", nana nana nana nana na na na "Micky Van de Ven, Van de Ven, Micky Van de Ven." And, of course, the Ange remake of Angels, "I'm loving big Ange instead." We sang along until we were hoarse, then sang and danced some more.

An inflatable trophy with Europa League winners printed on the front did the rounds. In truth, it looked nothing like the actual trophy, but nobody cared. We took it in turns to imitate Sonny, shaking the trophy towards the ground before slowly beginning to raise it, then launching it above our heads to a roar of approval.

It was a truly joyous event, proof of what I had been talking to Cam about that morning. The power of football to bring people together and create shared moments we will talk about for years to come.

As some of the more hardy revellers headed for the bars of Sydney, Tracy and I walked back across town to our Airbnb, made a cup of tea and put our feet up. It had been an emotionally draining day.

Sunday saw the conclusion of the National, including the AGM, a Spurs quiz, live music from former OzSpurs' president PAF's band 'Substation X' and, at 1am on Monday morning, a viewing of the last game of the season. Tracy and I were both feeling under the weather and left to take to our bed before the game kicked off. Watching it in the morning, I was glad we had.

Monday, 26th May 2025. Hyde Park Plaza, Sydney, NSW.

Premier League: Tottenham Hotspur 1 Brighton and Hove Albion 4

The bookies had Spurs at 5-1 to win this game, a price that

drifted from 4–1 a couple of days previously when it was clear how hard the Spurs players had been partying. An open-top bus tour saw an estimated 225,000 people turn out, a reminder of the huge supporter base the club commands.

Ange put out a strong team with only Romero, Bissouma and Richarlison replaced from the triumphant Bilbao starting lineup. The latter was replaced by Tel, who started enthusiastically and won a penalty on 17 minutes, duly dispatched by Solanke. Over the rest of the half Spurs were slowly pushed back into a defensive mode, not dissimilar to what we saw in the final.

With many of the players visibly tiring, the second half was always going to be a long one. In the end, it was one-way traffic and, unlike Manchester United a few nights before, Brighton had no difficulty breaking through the Spurs defence. Goals in the 51st, 64th, 88th and 93rd minutes saw a predictably miserable end to the Premier League campaign.

And then finally, sitting nursing a cold in an Airbnb overlooking a sunny Hyde Park on an autumn Sydney morning, it was all over. The end of a miserable and yet glorious season, possibly the most bizarre in the club's history. Spurs lost twice as many Premier League games as they won, but ended with only a minus one goal difference. Week after week I had watched us capitulate to less revered teams with more guile, quality and finesse than that displayed by my team.

But that day wasn't about football.

On Monday 26th May 2025, at the Chris O'Brien Lifehouse, a life ended. Surrounded by friends, family, love and the Spurs regalia left over from Thursday morning, one of our own, our 'Commander', departed. With dignity, courage and grace.

I will never forget my last moments with Cam, on Saturday morning.

As I took his hand, I thanked him for everything.

"Look after yourself," he said. I turned towards the door. "Love you, mate."

"Love you, mate," I replied, and left him for the last time.

Epilogue

My ambition, when embarking on this narrative, was to track my travels and my emotions as I followed Spurs through the season. Writing a book as a contemporaneous record of events, not knowing how it would end and what would happen along the way, seemed like an interesting idea. I knew our travels would see me watching matches in a diverse range of circumstances, although I never would have imagined the journey would take me into television punditry, or a cancer hospital.

The emotional journey of following Spurs this season turned out to be a torrid one. Opening up to vulnerability and repeatedly being let down is a form of abuse. In retrospect, I reverted to my defence mechanism and became apathetic, emotionally disengaged. Often I mentioned to people that I was thinking of giving up documenting the season, but they would always say "what if we end up with a trophy? That'll make it all worthwhile." So I persisted, and the trophy duly arrived, just as I predicted at the outset.

My reaction to the glorious victory in Bilbao was more muted than for many other Spurs fans. I did a bit of jumping around and hugging, but there were no tears. Just a deep and lingering sense of satisfaction. Maybe that's because the season wore me down. Or maybe it's because I was there to see Ricky Villa score the cup final winner in 1981, and present at the UEFA cup final in 1984. For me, those experiences will never be surpassed. But I enjoyed seeing the younger Spurs fans experience the joy. After seventeen long years, they deserved it.

Along the way, I have pondered what it means to be a football fan. Why does it seem to matter so much? The answer, I found, lies in the collective experience. My personal emotional journey is of little relevance. It is the huge global Spurs community, sharing through social media, podcasts and in person at supporters club meet-ups all over the world, that brings meaning. Life is about human connection.

My Spurs family is OzSpurs. A diverse collective of fans from all over Australia who enjoy friendship and offer support to each other. This was more clear at the end of this season than ever before. It was a group of people bound by a curious mix of joy and grief.

That is why, in the end, it wasn't the winning of a trophy that made the story of the season worth telling. It was something far more important. The power of football to create friendships that are deep and enduring.

Come on you Spurs!

In Ange we... oh, hang on a minute... what's that I just heard?

Also by Andrew Pettifer

If you enjoyed this book, you'll love *Travels with Tracy*, Andrew and Tracy's midlife gap year stories. Two Spurs fans, a bucket list and the world to explore.

Available now wherever you bought this book, or simply scan the QR code.

Follow Andrew on social media:

- 🌐 andrewpettifer.com
- 📷 andrew_pettifer_writes
- (X) @andrewpettifer
- ♪ @andrew.pettifer

Acknowledgements

Writing and publishing this book was a voyage of discovery. Enjoyable, at times traumatic, moving and ultimately immensely rewarding. I would like to thank the many people who helped me along the way.

Everyone at OzSpurs, a wonderfully supportive community. If I named one I would have to name all, so I offer a collective thanks.

Jack Pitt-Brooke and Alasdair Gold, for so readily weighing in to help promote the book.

Brendan McGerty and everyone at The Cheeseroom podcast, for going above and beyond with their support.

Steve Giblett and Martin Jopson, my personal editors and proofreaders, who spotted all my mistakes.

Sara Walker and everyone at Chris O'Brien Lifehouse, a wonderful institution and worthy beneficiary.

Jessica Mudditt and the Hembury Books team, for guiding me through the process with dedication and enthusiasm for the cause.

My Tottenham born Mum and lifelong Spurs fan Dad, for making me who I am.

My 'kids' George and Anna, for their love and support. Anna designed my personal logo and taught me how to use TikTok to promote the book, proving you can teach an old dog new tricks.

And last but certainly not least, my wonderful and indomitable wife Tracy, who joined me on this crazy journey following Spurs. We travel well together...

About the Author

Andrew Pettifer is a British-Australian author whose work explores the quirks of the human condition, the joys of travel, and a lifelong devotion to Tottenham Hotspur Football Club.

Born and raised in London, Andrew enjoyed a 35-year career as a chartered building services engineer, holding senior roles with global firms Arup and Mott MacDonald after relocating to Sydney in 2007. Throughout his working life, he cultivated an interest in leadership, human behaviour and storytelling. He has written extensively for the engineering industry, with articles published in The Fifth Estate and the CIBSE Journal.

In 2023, Andrew retired to pursue his passion for travel, sport and writing. With career ambitions fulfilled and a shared desire to live life to the full, he embarked on a midlife gap year with his wife Tracy that took them across five continents and every state in Australia. These journeys – filled with humour, insight and a fascination for people and places – inspired his travel memoir *Travels with Tracy*.

Andrew's writing invites readers to reflect on their own stories, embrace new adventures at any age, and find meaning in life's unpredictability. With a talent for finding humour in everyday moments, he shares tales of reinvention and resilience – and the emotional rollercoaster of following Tottenham Hotspur for over sixty years.

Printed in Dunstable, United Kingdom